LEGENDS FROM THE LOCKER ROOM

LEGENDS FROM THE LOCKER ROOM

HERB APPENZELLER

CAROLINA ACADEMIC PRESS
Durham, North Carolina

Library of Congress Cataloging-in-Publication Data

Names: Appenzeller, Herb, author.
Title: Legends from the locker room / by Herb Appenzeller.
Description: Durham, North Carolina : Carolina Academic Press, LLC
  [2019]
Identifiers: LCCN 2019024864 | ISBN 9781531015381 (paperback) |
  ISBN 9781531015398 (ebook)
Subjects: LCSH: Appenzeller, Herb. | Coaches (Athletics)—North
  Carolina—Biography. | Sports—North Carolina--History. |
  Athletes—North Carolina—Biography. | Wake Forest College.
Classification: LCC GV697.A67 A3 2019 | DDC 796.092 [B]—dc23
LC record available at https://lccn.loc.gov/2019024864

Carolina Academic Press
700 Kent Street
Durham, North Carolina 27701
Telephone (919) 489-7486
Fax (919) 493-5668
www.cap-press.com

DEDICATION

It is almost impossible to dedicate a book in a few sentences to someone who made the book possible. Ann Terrill Appenzeller saved my life on four occasions and then made my life worth living. She encouraged me to write Love (*Legends*) *in the Locker Room* when she believed the stories needed to be told. Whenever I started to give up she refused to let me get discouraged, and her inspiration and caring nature helped me achieve the goal of completing the book. She set the bar high and through her I have completed the book.

HTA

CONTENTS

ACKNOWLEDGMENTS

Upon the completion of each of my books, I have been careful to recognize those who have helped me in the process. I am always thankful for Carolina Academic Press and owners Keith and Linda Sipe, who both developed the sport management series in my name and became close friends. And to my wife, Ann, who is my promoter, supporter, encourager, pusher and soul mate.

But this time I must also recognize the person who has done the most to help me in every way to get *Legends from the Locker Room* ready for publication — Daniel Southard.

Ann calls him our godsend. We were both struggling with the completion of this book, primarily due to health issues. We felt that it would be useful to have someone who could help us with researching, writing and typing the manuscript. In addition, we needed someone who could help me with my diabetes and give Ann relief when needed.

One morning Ann saw an ad in our neighborhood online newspaper for a young man who was interested in working with a person who had health care needs. He had a college degree, having majored in English at Appalachian State University. In addition, he had experience in the medical and healthcare fields. Ann ran to the office and said, "Here is someone who could be a godsend for us!" Once she shared the information, including the fact that he was the son of Mike Southard, who is our webmaster, we called him for an interview.

I think we overwhelmed Daniel at first — me talking about the need to finish the book and Ann asking about his ability to work with a diabetic, who by that time had had two leg amputations. The kicker was that Daniel had absolutely no knowledge or interest in sport! Fortunately, we hired him and began a happy, satisfying relationship.

HTA

Addendum by Ann:

In the fall of 2017 I had emergency surgery, resulting in a 30-day hospital stay. During that time I had to find 24/7 assistance for Herb, in addition to Daniel. However, Daniel was the key — sharing his knowledge and experience with the home health caretakers—and he was always on call to help, as he lived only one neighborhood away!

Unfortunately, soon after returning from the hospital, I fell and broke my shoulder, wrist and hand, and once again Daniel was a godsend in working with Herb on the book.

Sadly, Herb passed away on January 5, 2018 from a heart attack. I pledged that I would finish the book for Herb, and without Daniel I could not have done so. The book gave me a reason to go on every day, and Daniel, having spent so much time with Herb, knew where to find the finished chapters (all but one) and where to find and identify the many pictures.

As we all know, Herb loved to tell stories about his legends over and over and over — and since Daniel had not heard them before, he was a great audience for Herb. So, with Daniel's help, I was able to complete the book that Herb wrote and Daniel and I compiled. What a godsend Daniel has been; I will be eternally grateful for his being.

ATA

PROLOGUE

"Stories and legends, as nothing else can do, reveal what is important to an institution."

—THOMAS PETERS and NANCY AUSTIN,
A Passion for Excellence

The word legend conjures up certain events and even names of famous people. Arnold Palmer is an example. However, this book is not about the types of legends most people recognize. The majority of the legends contained in this book, I witnessed during my career. I personally saw how players came together and triumphed in their own sport. Those, as the above quote says, revealed what is important to me—they are the highlights of my career in sports.

The definition of a legend, from Merriam Webster's dictionary, is "a person or thing that is very famous for having special qualities or abilities."[1] Many legends in this book will revolve around outstanding athletes and others that have special qualities and abilities. However, sports legends are not just people that accomplished a lot of wins or scores. They are people who achieved something outstanding or were outstanding in spite of their wins and losses. These legends, after reading about them in this book, could change your definition of a legend.

For example, one Guilford freshman women's tennis player from Finland won 31 matches in a season and lost none, gaining international attention for the feat. Those types of players and people are easy to count as legends. On the other side of the spectrum, a local legend at Guilford College named Coach Charles "Block" Smith, who coached during Guilford's early days, from 1937–1942, had a record achievement of having only 6 wins and 109 losses during his whole coaching career! That number combines the three different sports that he coached at Guilford, basketball, football, and baseball! Winners and losers are both considered legends in this book.

The above quote from the book *A Passion for Excellence* displays my belief that stories and legends are significant—not only to an institution but also to a person's life.

For years I have had a desire to share the events that affected my career in teaching and coaching. A few years ago my granddaughter, Sarah Somers, one of four granddaughters, called with a request. Sarah asked me to tell her about my early days, going back to my childhood. Then 91 years of age, I realized that my grandchildren and great grandchildren knew very little about my life. Sarah did not know about what I had accomplished.

These are reflections on my long career as a coach, teacher, and athletics director. Yet it is also the story of the many times I spent and shared with my athletes in the locker room. There is something magical about the locker room, just ask any coach or player. There is a bond that exists between players and their coaches that is special, which carries them through hardship, challenge, or triumph.

The bond that is forged through struggle, determination, wins, losses, and brave deeds is not easily forgotten. I can testify, many years later, that I can still vividly recall the moments of celebration and of sorrow in the locker room when the players and coaches came together. Many players, upon leaving a sport, will say that the thing they will miss the most is the camaraderie and the lasting friendship they felt in the locker room. My original title for this book was "Love in the Locker Room," by which I meant a brotherly love for one's teammates. My grandson Justin Appenzeller, one of my seven grandsons, thought it might be more politically correct to say "Legends from the Locker Room."

Several early events made a mark on my life, including the Hindenburg explosion and the coming of WWII. I remember I was playing softball as a boy in a community game in my hometown of Newark, New Jersey when the Pride of Germany, the Hindenburg used as propaganda for the Nazis, came so close to the ground that I felt I could almost touch the giant airship. The airship exploded minutes later as it attempted to land several miles away. Then came World War II, and the bombing of Pearl Harbor, which shocked the nation. I felt the effects of racism and the reverberations of the Holocaust because I was attending a predominantly Jewish high school during this time period. After Pearl Harbor, I felt called to volunteer for the military, but was turned down by the recruiters for a medical condition.

At that disappointing time several people suggested that I apply to colleges and universities, since there was a shortage of men to play sports. I sent letters to several universities, one of which was Wake Forest. The head football coach at Wake Forest, Douglas "Peahead" Walker, asked me to send two clippings of my high school sports achievements. I did, one in track and one in football. My track clipping was a story about how I got second place in the district championship in the 100 meter dash, despite having a dislocated elbow, wearing a heavy cast and taking a standing start! The second clipping was of my first varsity football game, where I took the kickoff and ran it down to the nine yard line. I did myself proud in that game as evidenced by my local newspaper, *The Star Ledger,* which included the headline: "Appenzeller on Rampage."

Coach Walker, upon reading those clippings, immediately contacted me and offered a full scholarship to Wake Forest to play football. I accepted and went to Wake Forest where I earned my B.A. (in Latin) and a M.A. (in Education). I accepted and left for Wake Forest College in 1943—the first person in my family to go to college. I rode the long bus ride from New Jersey and arrived in Wake Forest, North Carolina. At that time integration was in play. I rode in the back of the bus because I wanted to sleep! As we crossed the famous Mason-Dixon Line, the bus driver stopped the bus and told me to come to the front of the bus. A lesson learned early as I left the North, never to return.

Later I completed my Ed.D. at Duke University with the rare major or minor in Latin in all three degrees. William R. Rogers, retired Guilford College President, was pleased to say that his athletics director majored in Latin!

Later while teaching education I always expected my students to have their own philosophy of education. I have enjoyed my years of teaching with a philosophy that was written long ago by the Roman philosopher Quintilian, "Education is not what you can remember but the things you cannot forget."[2]

My career was a long one, spanning 41 years, as a teacher, coach, and athletics director, and co-writing the first textbook on sport management in the field. I have written 28 books, this being the 29th, and conducted risk reviews for sport facilities nationwide as well as serving as an expert witness in many legal cases.

Many of the stories that follow are more like miracles than actual true stories. Be assured, however, the stories are true and had a tremendous impact on my life, and I hope they will inspire others.

HERB APPENZELLER
Jefferson-Pilot Professor of Sport Studies, Emeritus,
Guilford College
January 2018

RESOURCES

1. https://www.merriam-webster.com/dictionary/legend
2. *Pride in the Past*, Herb Appenzeller, p. 82.

LEGENDS FROM THE LOCKER ROOM

CHAPTER 1

:::::

THE EARLY DAYS

I was born and raised in Newark, New Jersey, where I went to Madison West for Junior High. It was there I got my first opportunity to run track. I ran the 60-yard dash, and found out I was fast! The coaches made track fun, and we looked forward to it every day. In the first track meet I ever ran, I got second place! I was very excited and happy to get a medal. I also played football in Junior High and loved it.

WEEQUAHIC HIGH SCHOOL

One of my best friends and I wanted to go to Westside High School, but we were turned down, so we had to go to Weequahic High, filled with the sons and daughters of doctors and lawyers. However, it turned out to be a blessing in disguise. The rigorous nature of Weequahic High really helped me when I went to Wake Forest College (now University); it was so highly academic that it prepared me well for college. The principal there was Max Herstburg, known nationally for his work in mythology. The vice principal was Ms. Galligher, an Irish woman who ran the school.

Not only was the academic side important for preparing me for college, but so was the athletic side. I played football as a halfback, ran track, and played baseball as a catcher. I really enjoyed sports. I had good coaches, and they made it fun to play.

On November 11, 1941, Veteran's Day, Weequahic High School played its inner-city rival, South Side High School, in football. Both teams were located in Newark, New Jersey, and all of their home games were played in Newark's City Stadium. A large crowd attended the rivalry game, and several unexpected things happened that made the game memorable to all who were present. First, South Side came on the field, to the surprise of everyone, with brand-new plastic helmets. Weequahic players were shocked and intimidated by the shiny, gold helmets because all teams were wearing leather helmets at the time, and no one expected what they saw that day. Second, and most important, Walter Eisele, an outstanding defensive halfback, received a hard blow to the head as he tackled a Weequahic runner and was knocked unconscious. He was taken by ambulance to a nearby hospital and died three days later from a cerebral hemorrhage. Eisele's death stunned football players across the state of New Jersey. On the day after the fatal injury, a photo in the Newark Star Ledger showed Eisele making the tackle with his helmet turned sideways due to an improper fit.[1] This single event influenced the direction of my career — keeping players safe while averting lawsuits.

WORLD WAR II

Because of the bombing of Pearl Harbor, there was a huge wave of patriotism in the country, especially among the young men who wanted to go to war. I also felt called to go into service. However, both the Navy and the Army declined to accept me for military service due to a medical condition. While working briefly for the U.S. Postal Service, I felt more and more uncomfortable as I walked my route. There was almost a stigma if one did not go into the military at that time, and it was deeply embarrassing to be asked over and over why I as a young man was not in service, especially for me since it was due to an unforeseen medical condition that stopped me. Some would believe one was not patriotic if they did not go, others believed one was a coward for not going. It was a trying time for me in my life. In addition, the older carriers asked me to slow down. They had assigned me the most difficult route, up multiple flights of steps, and yet I was still finished long before they were!

APPLYING FOR COLLEGE

At this disappointing time in my life, several people suggested I apply to colleges and universities, since there was a shortage of men to play sports due to the draft. I sent letters to several institutions, asking for the opportunity to walk on the team and try out. One of those institutions was Wake Forest College in Wake Forest, North Carolina, now Wake Forest University in Winston-Salem, North Carolina.

NOTES

1. *Football Fatalities:1938 to 2011*, by Dr. Robert Cantu and Dr. Fred Mueller, Chapter 11.

CHAPTER 2

:::::

WAKE FOREST COLLEGE

When I first met Coach Walker, he was on the floor painting our leather helmets black. I was shocked to see the head football coach of a Division I school painting helmets. I will always appreciate Peahead Walker for putting me in Mrs. Sander's Boarding House with my first legend — Dewey Hobbs.

Dewey was a 6′2″, 230-pound tackle on our offensive and defensive lines. His head was so huge they had to make a special helmet for him! Dewey was studying to be a Baptist minister and as our spiritual leader attended Vespers every night. Dewey's leadership was felt all over the campus and his influence helped me.

One day a hardened group of students who lived off campus sent a challenge to come down and fight. Dewey told them to come meet us and we would be ready to fight. Once they saw him, and how huge he was, they took off!

On the field, Dewey had the total respect of our coach! We played the University of Miami (one time) and Dewey had a serious injury. His nose was severely broken as well as his teeth — he was a mess. Certainly, he would not be able to play or practice for a long time. However, to our surprise Peahead had gone to a nearby prison and had them make an iron facemask! Dewey did not miss a practice or game. As it turned out Dewey Hobbs be-

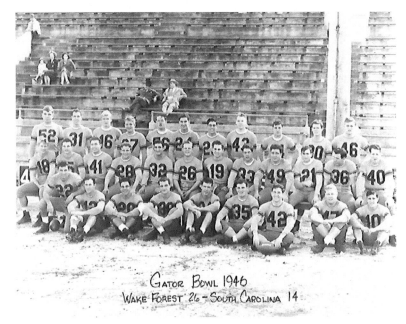

GATOR BOWL 1946
WAKE FOREST 26 – SOUTH CAROLINA 14

Dewey Hobbs is #52 and my number is #14 in the first Gator Bowl.

came the first person in Wake Forest history to wear a face mask and the only person in the Southern Conference.

We were in the Southern Conference at Wake Forest, and we had some talent on the team. My roommate, Richard Tate "Rock" Brinkley, was the leading fullback in the conference and made All Southern. "Rock" won a bunch of games for Peahead, he was that good. He was fullback, a big guy. He went into the pros on the Brooklyn Dodgers' football team.

THE ARMY GAME

I remember playing the Army team at West Point that wore the first plastic Riddell helmets in college football, which scared the leather helmet-wearing team from Wake Forest. Army was undefeated for three years running, and they ended up winning that game. It was the first time Peahead ever said to us before a game, "You aren't going to win this one. However you can tell your grandkids one day that you played the greatest team in college football." We were not interested in losing and telling our grandkids about it at that point!

THE FIRST GATOR BOWL

One of the highlights of being at Wake Forest was playing in the very first Gator Bowl, in 1946. It was Wake Forest vs. the University of South Carolina, and Wake Forest won, 26–14. I set a record that day, unintentionally. A South Carolina defensive back intercepted the ball I threw and ran it back 98 yards for a touchdown — a record that has never been broken in Gator Bowl history!

First Gator Bowl, Memorial Stadium, Jacksonville, Florida, January 1, 1946.
South Carolina vs. Wake Forest.

COACH "PEAHEAD" WALKER

Peahead was one of the most demanding and toughest coaches in the country. He was asked to speak at more banquets because he was funny and had many funny stories along with funny ties. One of our teammates' sisters still lived in New Jersey. Peahead took her out for dinner when he was recruiting in the area. The entire evening she called him "Pear-head." We rolled in the floor laughing when she told her brother.

Peahead had a tremendous impact on me. On one hand he disappointed me because I was the fastest runner on the team, and Peahead did not care a thing about track. I did run track, though, and actually got second place at a meet at the University of North Carolina that had great runners from all over the country and I lettered at William and Mary. Unfortunately, Peahead did not play me very much. I remember getting one touchdown, and it was only because *the team* gave me a chance during a game and I ran the football in for a touchdown.

We were undefeated one year, and went over to play Duke University in Durham. Peahead had a special play, where he could have used my speed as a halfback to make the play. I called my parents and asked them to come from New Jersey to North Carolina to watch me in that game because we had practiced that special play in preparation for the Duke game. However, Peahead never ran it. Peahead was a tough, gruff coach who cussed his players out regularly and did not seem to have a heart.

I determined that I would never coach the way Peahead coached, never! I would do my own way; right or wrong, I would do it differently. I did not want to be like him — his gruff, profane style was not the style I wanted to emulate, as a person or as a coach. Amazingly, I had many fellow teammates who later went on to become coaches who turned out just like Peahead! That surprised me, really. That was the way they thought they should coach. Peahead was successful, there was no question about that.

Coach "Peahead" Walker. I am Number 14 on the bench.

The reason was the majority of the players were really afraid of him. That's why they played so well.

Peahead really pushed his players — he was kind of a task master. For example: one of the players got a broken ankle and was sent to the health center on campus to be treated. When Peahead heard, he sent word that the player had better be at practice that day, or else lose his meal ticket for the dining hall that day (meaning he couldn't eat that day). The player came back to practice — and it was one of his star players! He had a lack of sympathy for injured players. Coach Walker expected them to be at practice, no matter what. It did not always work out that way, though. He kind of ran it like the military, which is a good

I am number 14, on the right at Wake Forest playing football
with two teammates.

comparison. During my first year I also experienced an injury during practice, and was moved to the side. After practice everybody went up the hill and left me lying there injured. I started crawling and finally met up with some of my buddies who took me to the health center.

OTHER LEGENDARY TEAMMATES
AT WAKE FOREST

"Red" Cochran was another outstanding player for Wake Forest. He later went on to play for the Green Bay Packers as a defensive back and later became a coach for them. When he died, they lowered the flag to half-mast in his honor — the first player ever honored that way.

Mac Grandy is an interesting story, because he was the first player who ever sued Peahead. He got hurt during one game, and was lying on his back in the rain and there was no team doctor that day. Because of that, Mac sued Peahead, and lost his case and became a lawyer after that!

MY MEMORIES OF ARNIE THE "KING"

I remember the day I first saw Arnold Palmer hitting practice balls on the back nine of the old Wake Forest golf course. It was 1946, and having just completed a rugged spring football practice, I picked up three clubs from the fieldhouse to play a few holes. There was this new student out there hitting ball after ball, but never playing a single hole. I couldn't imagine why someone would just hit balls without playing. It was Arnold Palmer, before he became famous.

After not winning an ACC golf tournament for several seasons, our athletics director, Jim Weaver, funded five scholarships for golf and found places in the Colonial Club for them to live. Among those recruited were Bud Worsham and his best friend Arnold Palmer from Latrobe, Pennsylvania. As they began to win tournaments, the Wake students became excited and the Deacon golfers were on their way. Unfortunately Worsham was killed in an automobile accident and Palmer left soon after to join the U.S. Coast Guard for three years.

When Arnie returned to Wake Forest after WWII, the Deacons began again to win tournaments and conference championships as Weaver had predicted. Wake Forest golf became a national power.

At the famed Masters Golf Tournament in Augusta, Georgia, a local newspaperman named the large contingency following Palmer "Arnie's Army." Years later I became one of "Arnie's Army" at the Greater Greensboro Open when the PGA annually came to Greensboro. When Arnie acquired his first million dollar jet I went to the local airport to admire it. Later on the 13th tee at Sedgefield he looked over at me with the recognition of an old

Wake Forest student-athlete. He never forgot his alma mater. He hosted a tournament each year for Wake Forest golf alums who were on the tour.

In 2000 my son, Tom, a college coach, was thrilled when Arnold Palmer autographed a picture to give me, one of his last. Winnie Palmer, his wife, was a furniture designer, designing many of the pieces in their home. One of my wife Ann's favorites was the Arnold Palmer desk, which is a tall desk used by architects and designers. I gave one of the last desks designed by Winnie to Ann for helping me with my writing and her decorating business! With several pictures from my son and her desk we have a shrine to Arnie in our office.

My career, sport management, was influenced by Palmer. He formed, along with his agent Mark McCormack, IMG, the first company for sport marketing and Arnie, his client, became the first professional golfer to earn a million dollars. I developed the academic field of sport law and sport management at Guilford College and consulted with other colleges and universities to develop their sport law and risk management programs influenced by IMG as well as the academic program at the University of Massachusetts.

Several years ago Arnold asked to meet some of his friends at Shorty's Grill on the old campus in the town of Wake Forest. He asked that a message be sent that he would arrive at Shorty's at noon. True to his word the door to Shorty's opened and Arnold walked in at 12 noon. I was fortunate enough to have an invitation, as were those in the enthusiastic crowd.

When legendary football coach "Peahead Walker" at Wake Forest retired to Charlotte, he called Dave Harris, his 1947 All Southern team captain as well as captain of the first Gator Bowl. He asked him over for a steak and when Dave looked around the room he realized there was only one picture on the wall — that of Arnold Palmer. Dave asked him where were the pictures of his football players and Coach Walker answered, "That is my fool's

Arnold Palmer

picture. Every day before practice I would put on my shoes as Arnold would pass by with his golf shoes and I would call over to him, 'Why don't you come out for football? I heard you were a top player, why not join us and become a NFL player where you could make a fortune.' So that is my fool's picture, and I was the fool."

In 2006 Wake Forest football was fortunate to win the Atlantic Coast Conference title and play Louisville in the Orange Bowl. How appropriate it was to have the two "Kings" representing their alma maters at the coin toss, Arnold Palmer for Wake Forest and Muhammed Ali representing Louisville, both of whom passed away ten years later in 2016.

The British playwright who authored *Peter Pan* wrote, "God gives us memories so that we can have roses in December." What a bouquet of roses were seen in that cathedral in Pennsylvania, where Arnold was eulogized by business friends, college friends, and most of the golfing world.

GRADUATION

I had a lot of fun at Wake, and made good friends. I earned my Bachelor of Arts in Latin, with a minor in English. After graduation I needed a job, so I applied for and was accepted into my first teaching and coaching job at Rolesville High school in the small town of Rolesville, North Carolina, not far from the Wake Forest campus. Little did I know that I would encounter two more legends while coaching in that tiny rural town.

CHAPTER 3

:::::

A SPECIAL TIME AND PLACE:
ROLESVILLE HIGH

I graduated from Wake Forest in January of 1948 with a degree in Latin and a minor in English. Coaching and teaching jobs were scarce after the War. There was a vacancy at Rolesville High School for a coach, athletics director and teacher position. I got the job and was hired to start the spring semester. As a teacher I taught 8th grade in all subjects, but not Latin!

I chose to coach the boys' basketball and baseball teams over the girls', even though the girls had a better record than the dismal 3–13 of the boys.

OSCAR T. BARHAM

We had one of the most outstanding athletes at Rolesville High School — his name was Oscar T. Barham (or "O. T." for short). He was a tremendous athlete, and one that led the basketball team to win 13 games in a row as well as the conference championship!

WEATHER MAKES A DIFFERENCE!

The day before I started my coaching job, I watched Rolesville High play with a "give and go" attack against a tight zone that stole the ball one time after another. This had to change!

A heavy snowstorm blew through, causing the school to be closed for over a week. This gave me the time to put in a zone offense that had potential. I picked my players up for two weeks and put a zone offense in to replace the man-to-man offense against a zone.

When school started again the team was coachable and became excited about the rest of the season. Rolesville was ready to play and won all the games before the conference playoffs but one. The former losing team went from a 3–13 record to 13–3.

EFFECT OF OSCAR T. ON THE BASKETBALL TEAM

I was also a rookie basketball coach at Rolesville High. It was my first year coaching ever. Oscar T. knew my reputation from Wake Forest, and he talked to my other players and got them to trust and believe in me. His attitude helped me gain the confidence of the team. At times when we got behind during a game, he assured the team not to worry and he upped the ante and led them to victory.

That first season, we won all but one game. The reason we lost that game was I changed the lineup and we were defeated by Wendell High, but the next night we defeated Wendell.

We went on to play for the conference championship against Cary of the Western division, in a nail-biting finish in Gore Gym on the now old Wake Forest campus. Our team won the conference championship by one point! It was a miracle! Oscar T. Barham was named MVP in the conference championship and led all scorers.

Rolesville basketball team, 1948. O. T. Barham is #4
on the bottom right.

BASEBALL AT ROLESVILLE

O. T. also starred on my baseball team. He played the position of shortstop. Oscar T. could also pitch really well, and I believed he had the potential to be a major league baseball pitcher, so I told his father I would save his arm by putting him in at shortstop. O. T. led the team in hitting, pitching and fielding. He talked to the baseball team, and helped give them confidence in my ability to lead them as a baseball coach as well.

One game was against Coach Ennis of Red Oak High School, who went on to win many titles in the state of North Carolina. Bill Ennis was a classmate of mine at Wake Forest, had won the baseball conference championship the year before and was leading the conference when we played them this particular game.

Coach Ennis told me before the game that he heard I had a great pitcher who had a great fastball. I smiled and said, "You are right but I'm saving his arm and I play him at shortstop." Ennis told me he hoped O. T. would pitch because his men loved to hit a fastball. He said this as a challenge. In the seventh inning, the score was 1–0, with Rolesville ahead. I wanted to win this rivalry game and decided to put O. T. in the game. Oscar T. then struck out seven men in a row and we won the game. Needless to say, Coach Ennis saw O. T. in action and knew all he heard about O. T. was true for all to see.

O. T. Barham led Rolesville to a strong record and we won the baseball conference, with him starring in the field and at bat. Once again he qualified for MVP as the best conference athlete. The Wake Forest and Rolesville area all knew the exploits of Oscar T. Barham, who became a living legend and helped me win two conference championships my first year as a coach! Unbelievable!

IMPACT OF OSCAR T.

Oscar T. proved to me that a country boy with ability and character could become a legend. Same for his cousin, Franklin "Shorty" Barham. The words I would use to describe Oscar T. later on were "cocky but lovable."

Both men had the desire to prove that they were good. If you have character and good people around you, you can succeed. It does not matter your background: rich, poor, whatever; if you have character and desire you can lead a team.

THE REST OF OSCAR T.'S STORY, OR WHATEVER HAPPENED TO OSCAR T.?

"O. T.", as he was called, had a full baseball and basketball scholarship to Wake Forest College. However he turned it down after taking one religion class that bewildered him. He did not think he could pass the classes. When he left Wake he would hide in the woods when he saw my car coming. Instead, he decided to sign a minor league contract with the Yankees. At the end of the year, O. T. was voted the Minor League's MVP and Rookie of the Year.

FRANKLIN "SHORTY" BARHAM

Franklin "Shorty" Barham was Oscar T. Barham's cousin. He was also on the basketball and baseball teams with Oscar T., and was himself a good athlete, although I did not know it when I first met him. However, one night at a basketball game he proved his worth to the entire crowd for his athletic ability.

A Friday night in our first conference game against Garner High School, the "top team in the West" the Western Division of Wake County, North Carolina, which was coached by my college roommate, "Rock" Brinkley, found us in the role of underdog. We could not stop one of their guards who was too fast.

I turned to a man on the bench and asked who was the fastest man on our team. The answer was quick —"Franklin Barham (Shorty), at the end of the bench, a freshman who never plays."

I surprised Shorty by putting him in the game and it was almost a miracle. He was all over the court — guarding the fast player from Garner High School and stealing the ball and scoring points.

He became the star to everyone's surprise. Together, he and Oscar T. Barham had a field day and we won, with O. T. and Franklin starring, scoring points and stealing the ball, easily defeating Garner High School. Shorty, due to his ability and speed, won the next four games for Rolesville.

BASKETBALL CONFERENCE
CHAMPIONSHIP

The duo led the Rolesville High School team and faced Cary High for the opportunity to play them for the championship of Wake County. It was hard to believe when we won the conference championship against Cary, the largest school in the conference. Shorty and his cousin Oscar T. Barham starred as we won in Gore Gymnasium. O. T. was voted MVP and Shorty was runner-up in the voting. His athletic ability, along with Oscar T.'s, helped me win my first basketball conference championship.

ONE FUNNY STORY

Shorty Barham was also a baseball catcher for the Rolesville team. Our team really liked it when New York Yankee outfielder "Bud" Metheny, my favorite player from the New York Yankees, came to play Rolesville as the coach of Old Dominion's baseball team. "Bud" would bring his team over to Rolesville to scrimmage our team. We would play his team in a friendly game. One day Bud Metheny got tired of us winning and we had an incident that almost led to a bitter fight.

Both teams would get a player to call the game as umpire. We knew they were calling the game for fun. On this day, we played Old Dominion University and for some reason Old Dominion was tense and on edge. The game was close and we were one run behind.

Our umpire was one of our Rolesville players, a gigantic tackle from football season. Old Dominion was behind by one run and they were upset to be down one run in the ninth inning. Old Dominion got a man on base and felt they could go into an extra inning and tie the game. With a man on third base, Old Dominion knew they could tie the game with a hit. Suddenly, Old Dominion was excited about tying the score.

An Old Dominion player hit the ball over the shortstop's head and the man on third base was going in to score to tie the game. The ball came to third base and the Old Dominion player ran into home.

Suddenly the student umpire hollered to Shorty, Rolesville's catcher, "He missed third base, Shorty, go get him!" Shorty retrieved the ball and quickly tagged the runner out. The Old Dominion player was incensed over the call.

A serious fight erupted and fists flew. The fight lasted too long and the umpire called the game. I finally got them to calm down, but that strained our once-good relationship with Bud Metheny. (Note: It took a delay of several years for the two teams to play again but only when proper officials called the games. Shorty went to Chowan College with me when I later took the coaching job there.)

ON TO WAKELON HIGH

After two special years at Rolesville High School, I accepted the position of athletics director and football, basketball and baseball coach at Wakelon High in Zebulon, North Carolina. My principal, Fred A. Smith, paid me the highest coaching supplement in Wake County — $1,000 a year, which was a decent amount of money in those days!.

Later in my career there were only two people in the country who coached and taught Latin at the same time, and I was one of them! I do not know that other man's name, but he lived on the West Coast while I lived on the East Coast.

CHAPTER 4

:::::

AN UNLIKELY HERO:
THE BILLY PIPPIN STORY

When I took the job as teacher-coach at Wakelon High School, I saw a young boy who lived in a home for disabled children. He had stayed in the same classroom at Wakelon for his entire education, from first grade up. I quickly learned, however, that Billy Pippin loved to play baseball, even with his many physical and mental disabilities. Billy also loved his teacher, who worked with him for all those years at Wakelon. He was a good kid, quiet yet hard working.

With permission from his teacher and from all, I decided to let Billy practice with the baseball team and the football team every day, and his teammates welcomed him. He loved practice and we loved his enthusiasm.

One day, we were playing for the championship in baseball against a team that we thought we may not beat. The senior class went to Washington leaving only the second team and scrubs to play the game. For that reason I did not think there was much chance of winning. Having never played in a game that season, Billy approached me and asked if he could play. On that day, I began to feel that a loss might even be worth Billy's chance to play. With the bases loaded and down three runs, it was a pivotal moment in the game. Yet, I could not resist him, and let him put his cap on and march out onto the field to home plate. He put his bat on his shoulder and eagerly awaited the pitcher's throw. The whole crowd and I watched with bated breath.

The pitcher threw a fastball down the middle, and Billy hit it! The ball soared into the air, and Billy threw his bat down and ran for his life. The ball smacked the fence at the edge of the field. Amazingly, he hit a triple, allowing three runners to go to home, and had tied the game. He stopped running at third base, with the crowd cheering.

The game was not over yet. I called a time out and I went out and whispered something to Billy. The pitcher, thinking Billy had made a lucky hit, failed to pay attention to Billy, who was biding his time at third base. When the pitcher was not looking in his direction, Billy made a beeline for home plate. By the time the pitcher recovered, Billy had stolen home! This broke the tie and we won the game, all thanks to Billy Pippin. The team streamed out of the dugout and gathered around Billy. They picked him up on their shoulders and carried him around the field in celebration. The crowd went wild!

BILLY'S LEGACY

Billy became a local hero due to that game. His love for the game and his performance that day inspired the people in the town, and they came to regard him as a local legend. He was indeed a most unlikely hero. His life changed dramatically. People would see him on the street and clap him on the back for what he did, and praise him and praise him.

I later wrote about Billy's story and it was accepted for publication in the book *Chicken Soup for the Teacher's Soul* in 2001. His story has inspired others, some of whom wrote to me and told me how his story helped them with their own children with disabilities have hope that if Billy could do it, so could they.

Billy Pippin shocked me that day. The reason I let him on the team was because I wanted to get him out of that one room; I saw things in him, and knew he could play if given the chance.

The story of Billy Pippin will go down in the school's history for his remarkable achievement in a championship game. His life has influenced the lives of others struggling with a disability by showing that they, too, can succeed and overcome. The history of both Rolesville and Wakelon is a like a storybook, an incredible time. Billy Pippin's life is a heart-warming story — hard to believe but true.

CHAPTER 5

:::::

During the summer when I was not teaching at Rolesville and Wakelon, I was able to complete my master's degree in education and physical education from Wake Forest, graduating with my master's in 1951. From there I went to Chowan College in Murfreesboro, North Carolina, to coach and teach.

When I went to Chowan College (now University), the president of the college, Dr. Mixon, called me into his office one day before the start of my first year there. He asked me about the number of football players that came out that year for football. I told him that only nine came out, so we would not have a team. However, I assured him I would have 35 ready to play next year.

He said, "Next year? There will not be a next year for this college if we do not have a football program."

Dr. Mixon told me that I should get enough men to play because the college was on the verge of closing and the people in town expected Chowan to close if we did not field a team.

With that news, I met with our team of nine that day and told them of the dire situation we faced. I told them to go home and bring back a friend or a family member that wanted to join our

Appenzeller "Eternal" Fountain, Chowan University

team. Nine went home that night, and the next day we had 19 ready to play for us! Each man had brought a friend or brother back with him, and one man brought two because a young man driving the ice cream truck said he wanted to join them! So he parked his truck on the side of the road and made up the 19th. It was a miracle! Though we were able to have a football team that year, we did not win the conference, but we won enough games to earn third place and keep the college alive.

I stayed at Chowan for a total of five wonderful years. Going to Chowan turned out to be one of the best things that could have happened to me. I felt very strongly at the time I was supposed to be there.

A few years ago, the university honored me by naming an eternal fountain in the university lake the Appenzeller Fountain. There is a stone plaque in front of the fountain that reads:

> *The Lake Fountain expresses appreciation*
> *to Herbert Appenzeller, the College's*
> *first director of athletics from*
> *1951 to 1956. As physical education teacher*
> *and coach of football, basketball,*
> *baseball and track, his recruitment*
> *efforts helped the college to remain*
> *open at a critical time in its history.*

Chowan University is one of the fastest growing schools in North Carolina today.

HILLIARD GREENE

When I coached basketball at Wakelon High School in Zebulon, I got to be friends with a young man who worked for a local printing company. Hilliard Greene worked in the Zebulon Print Shop across the street from the Zebulon newspaper. He came across the road to the school gym every day to help me coach the high school boy's team. At 6'7", he could shoot better than any player on my team and impressed our players.

After getting to know him a little better, I found out that he had never been to college. He had graduated from Wakelon in

Hilliard Greene

1947, and had played football and basketball for them for three years. He had an impressive hook shot, taught to him by his high school coach, R. F. Lowry. Coach Lowry went to UNC when the famous basketball player "Hook" Dillon was there. After Lowry taught it to Hilliard, it became his favorite shot.

When I signed a contract to coach all three sports at Chowan College, I asked Hilliard if he would go to Chowan and help me in all three sports, but now as an athlete. He jumped at the chance to get a two year degree and play for me at Chowan College (now University).

Hilliard was one of those nine players that expanded the football team to nineteen. He played football, basketball and baseball with leadership skills. Although he was close to my age, he always called me Coach Appenzeller. We won almost all our games because of him, with basketball being his best sport. Hilliard won Player of the Year in the league the first year he and I were at Chowan.

Hilliard had many athletic accomplishments while at Chowan. He was the leading scorer on the 1952–53 basketball team. He was also voted conference Player of the Year in baseball. As an older, more mature student-athlete, Hilliard was also named MVP over Oak Ridge's, who was a recruited player at Wake Forest where he also starred in basketball. Hilliard also played wide receiver on the football team.

Just like at Rolesville and at Wakelon, our baseball and basketball teams won the conference championship that first year. I had really good men under my leadership, truly. They were great, both in their character and as players.

Hilliard Greene was a campus leader, a very good student. As a three sport letterman, he had a positive influence on the campus. He also accepted leadership in many roles, such as the men's vocal quartet.

In Hilliard's final game at Chowan, the University of North Carolina with its great freshmen came to play us. Their freshman team was very talented. They defeated the Chowan team 100–90. Hilliard scored a lot of points to become Chowan's leading scorer. UNC sent Charlie "Choo Choo" Justice to offer him a full athletic scholarship, which Hilliard accepted and went on to play basketball at UNC-Chapel Hill.

THE ALLIGOOD BROTHERS

When I coached baseball at Chowan College in the 1950s, I had two brothers from Washington, North Carolina, on the team. They were C. J. and Bobby Alligood. Both were exceptional pitchers who could play other positions as well. C. J. pitched for us whenever we needed to win an important baseball game. Bobby was a fullback in football as well as a pitcher, while C. J. played baseball only.

These super baseball pitchers helped Chowan College win the baseball championship in 1954. Troy Perry and Sam Evans joined the Alligood brothers as pitchers to help win the baseball championship. Chowan College won a double-header at Wingate junior college and Louisburg College two days later to clinch the conference championship. The strength of the pitching corps clinched the championship. C. J. Alligood was the All Conference pitcher.

At one game, I realized C. J. was having a difficult time. He was very tired, so I went to the mound to see what was wrong. "Coach," he said, "I am really tired, I have no energy and I doubt if I can pitch." I told C. J. I could handle it. I got several candy bars and gave them to him. He ate them and pitched a great game. He never forgot it. He always credited me after that for pitching so well after the candy bars, but I knew it was because he was a great pitcher, not because of anything I had done. He later kept a Hershey bar in his pocket during his games and never had a problem again.

C. J. made All Conference and All State in baseball. Bobby was a tough, determined football player and he helped us win the Conference title in 1954. We needed both brothers to win our first baseball championship at Chowan in 1954.

THE 1955 FOOTBALL TEAM

Chowan's 1955 team was my favorite team ever to coach. It was my last team I coached at Chowan. Men like the late Herman Clark, John Warren, Al Vaughn, Jim Gravely and Ted Rollins represented the best in Chowan College history. That team was legendary . . . and I consider the whole team together as a legend.

We did really well that season. We were playing our last game in football in 1955 against Bullis Prep, operated by the Navy, and they had one of the strongest teams we ever played against. They had players from some of the best schools in the country. That was the only game we lost. They switched up their offense that day, and we did not recover. We would have been undefeated, but as it stood it was 8–1.

My assistant coach, Paul Davis, and I said the 1955 team was the best team we ever coached. Our halfback Al Vaughn became All America. Without knowing it, I had recruited one of the finest in Chowan's sports history. Only four years after the college almost closed, our team did so well it was voted one of the two best teams in Chowan's football history. Unbelievable!

There were a number of good athletes on the 1955 team, men like Ben Rich, Jim Waverly, Jack Crenshaw, and Hardin Wood. C. J. Belch and Wayne Browning also were on that team. But there are two men who had a special impact on me and who I consider to be legends on the 1955 team. Those men were Ted Rollins and Albert Vaughn.

TED ROLLINS

I have fond memories of Ted Rollins — an outstanding man, tough as nails but with a warm heart of gold! He came to Chowan from Selma High School, where he was good. He showed he was willing to work and help how he could.

When he first came, he had a chip on his shoulder, because only a small two year school picked him. It hurt his feelings that a big school did not get him. But the more he hung around, the better he fit in, and gradually fell in love with the school and players. He "converted" until he was an asset to the team, and became a leader on the team. He also met Billy Pippen, and made a difference in Billy's life, and Billy made a difference in his life. Years later, his wife said, "You (Herb) have made a big difference in his life. He loves you, sir."

I remember the time Wake Forest came to play against our Chowan team — they were practicing against us to test some Canadian players they were recruiting. When they practiced with us, Ted Rollins was better than all of the Canadian players! After it was over, Wake Forest selected Ted Rollins and offered him a full football scholarship to Wake Forest University — which was my school, my alma mater! It meant a lot. Though I was not surprised because Ted was one of the best tackles I ever coached, and the offer to Wake Forest gave me a source of pride. At Chowan, Ted easily qualifies as a legend in my book.

ALBERT VAUGHN

We were having a great year in basketball at Chowan College. With Ken Haswell and Aubrey Edwards from Knightdale, both Wake County District Champions, we were a powerful team.

Albert Vaughn from Ahoskie, North Carolina, came to see me about coming to Chowan and getting a place on the basketball team. Here you find a potentially great player joining a great team. To be honest I was afraid Albert would break up the team with his shooting ability. It was already a great team and they had meshed well together. Albert loved to shoot the ball instead of passing it and being a team player, and I was afraid he would come in and mess up the team dynamic that already existed. So I turned him down.

Later, I realized my mistake. However, to his credit, Al Vaughn did not give up and the following year, 1955, he enrolled at Chowan and came out for football. In our opening game, Albert broke loose from tackles for several punt returns for touchdowns and looked great.

On Monday of the next week, I saw Albert coming toward me at practice. He was grinning as he approached me. I knew he was going to mention a scholarship but I beat him to it and gave him a grant-in-aid.

In basketball Al was a team player that year and a great player. Our team with Al won the conference and played North Greenville, South Carolina, for the right to go to the Nationals in Kansas City. North Greenville was undefeated until we defeated them at home. However, we lost the next two games in the playoffs and we went home. Albert made All State in football and basketball, but baseball was his best sport. With his help, we went to the conference championship and he made All State in baseball at second base.

His list of accomplishments is extraordinary. At Chowan he made All Conference, All District and All State in three sports: football, basketball, and baseball. His freshman year, Albert was named the school's "Outstanding Athlete." He also made All Academics, as well as All America. An outstanding player!

Albert's Legendary Career

Not only was Albert a great athlete, but he was one of the outstanding high school coaches in North Carolina. He coached the East team in the East-West All-Star football game. He also won many state titles while coaching in different sports. He was, in all probability, the outstanding athlete and coach in several sports, both at Chowan College and East Carolina.

Albert was great to coach, and we stayed in touch after he graduated from Chowan in 1957. He went to East Carolina University (ECU) to play baseball. Albert was later honored to be included in Chowan's Hall of Fame. He was the man responsible for designing the Hall of Fame rings at Chowan. While at ECU, Albert set the individual stolen base record that stood from 1959 until the late 1970s. He was named All Conference, All State, and NAIA All America.

Later he was elected to East Carolina's Hall of Fame as well. Albert only played two years at ECU! What an honor! Albert asked my wife Ann and me to attend his Hall of Fame ceremony. We are proud to name him a legend.

WAYNE BROWNING

Wayne Browning, known as "Red," was the outstanding lineman for the football team. Wayne was recognized when he starred for his two years on the team. Browning was a campus leader and led the team during the early years of football.

Wayne Browning excelled in all three sports at Chowan. Later, he got us uniforms when I was still at Chowan. We wore a different color uniform every year as I got football friends to give me their previous year's uniforms. Most people finished at Chowan while I was there not knowing what color the Braves really were.

CHAPTER 6

:::::

I moved to Guilford College in Greensboro, North Carolina, from Chowan in 1956. I knew about Guilford College being a very good school academically but that it had a sport program without much success.

HISTORY OF GUILFORD COLLEGE ATHLETICS

Guilford College had a rich history for being such a small private Quaker school. The first president of Guilford College, Lewis Lyndon Hobbs, is credited with bringing baseball to the South. Historians point to the game between Amherst and Williams (which Amherst won 56–32) in 1859 as the first intercollegiate baseball game in the history of the United States. Many sports historians believe, however, the game between New Garden Boarding School (later known as Guilford College) and the Greensboro team "Big Lazies" was the first baseball game in the South in 1868. They also believe the New Garden game against Oak Ridge in 1868 was the first interscholastic baseball game in the South.[1]

Guilford's first game as a college was against Oak Ridge Academy in 1889, and is claimed to be the first baseball game played in the state of North Carolina. A large crowd of pro-Guilford people came out and celebrated the game. Each pitcher struck out 21 batters with the score tied 6–6. The Guilford Quakers had great baseball under President Hobbs and his sons, the "Hobbs Hollow Boys" — Wilson, Louis, Richard, and Walter, that influenced the future of Guilford College athletics.[1]

In 1913, the Guilford baseball team was outstanding. When President Hobbs was to retire, he made sure that baseball would remain strong. He wrote, "we believe an impression has been made upon the students that will forever testify to the power and beauty and attractiveness of simple truth."[2]

The Hobbs Hollow Boys

The Hobbs Hollow Boys, the team President Hobb's sons were on, soon became legends in the South, and led to Guilford College's "Golden Age" in baseball in the early 1900s.[1] During this

Newspaper clipping of 1906 Guilford Baseball team,
the Hobbs Hollow Boys

time baseball was clearly the priority sport, but track and field were gaining popularity along with tennis and basketball. Football was the lone casualty and would continue to be a controversial subject on campus for many years.

The McBanes

Every so often a proud group of a talented family comes along to set records in sports. Grady and Edgar McBane were brothers, who did themselves proud at Guilford as athletes in the 1910s and 1920s.[3] Their first cousin Clyde and their father's first cousins Elwood and Everette ("Tom") were also outstanding Guilford athletes in multiple sports. Edgar ("Ed") was a coach for only one year in 1923, but his Pomona high school team won the state championship! He became a school principal for 17 years, and

Edgar McBane

Everette "Tom" McBane

earned a reputation for missing only one Guilford baseball game in 73 years of attendance. On Guilford College's campus, the baseball field is named McBane Field, in his honor. McBane Oil company is still in business in Greensboro today.

Ernie Shore

Guilford legend Ernie Shore led the Guilford pitching staff in those early days and won many games as a pitcher. Shore went to the pros as a pitcher for the New York Yankees and the Boston Red Sox, where he and Babe Ruth together pitched a "perfect game" in 1917. Before Babe Ruth became a famous batter, he was a pitcher. During this famous game, Babe Ruth walked the first man and then was ejected for throwing a punch at the umpire over a call. Shore came in as Babe Ruth's relief pitcher and proceeded to strike out the next 26 men in a row after the first base runner was thrown out attempting to steal. Ernie Shore went down in history as the only relief pitcher in a major league game to throw a perfect game.[4] Later he became the sheriff of Forsyth County in North Carolina. He was honored in the Guilford College Athletics Hall of Fame. The Wake Forest baseball field in Winston-Salem, North Carolina, was later named Ernie Shore Field in his honor.

Lucien Smith

Lucien Smith was outstanding as a pitcher and was much in demand at colleges. After enrolling at Oak Ridge he went to Guilford College and later Wake Forest College. After retiring from an injury, Lucien was the first baseball coach at Guilford College, part-time, while he farmed and served as a deputy sheriff in Guilford County.

Lucien was called "College Smith" by his teammates, because he had gone to college. Playing in New Orleans, his favorite team and city, Lucien was considered a wonderful twirler (Merriam-Webster defines a twirler as an apparently archaic term

Lucien Smith

for a pitcher).[5] "Without a doubt Smith, the wonderful young pitcher has again triumphed . . . beyond the shadow of a doubt, the boy is head and shoulders above the men in the Southern League, and this alone is a great compliment."* Two of Lucien's sons were coached by him: French H. Smith, who was a star at Guilford College, and the best-known son, Rufus "Shirt" Smith, a left handed pitcher for Jersey City. The third son was Jack Smith who was regarded as one of the best basketball players in the state at that time.

Rick, Wes, and George Ferrell

In 1924 Rick Ferrell started playing baseball at Guilford College for the first time, and three years later he was joined by his brother Wes. Both became highly successful in major league baseball. along with Rufus "Shirt" Smith. There was also a third Ferrell, George. He played before Rick and Wes and chose to stay home to take care of his family rather than join the major leagues. George became the best minor league player in history according to baseball buffs.

RUFUS "SHIRT" SMITH

Rufus Smith, a son of Lucien Smith, described himself as an errand boy, a professional baseball player, a construction superintendent, cotton gin operator, farmer, home builder, merchant and rental property developer. He played on several pro-

Newspaper clipping of Rufus Smith

fessional teams, including one coached by the late Casey Stengel, who made the Baseball Hall of Fame as the famous manager of the New York Yankees.

Rufus related one humorous story while playing for Detroit. While there, he witnessed a big old outfielder named "Fatty" Fothergill. This man could really hit but was one of the worst fielders he ever saw. He was playing in Boston and they had a short left field that ended against a high wall and "Fatty" was playing that day. Rufus said late in the game a Boston batter hit a fly ball into the wall, and Fothergill, the outfielder, and the ball arrived at the same time. The force of Fothergill slamming into the wall snapped his belt and his pants fell down. Smith said that was one of the funniest sights he ever saw on a baseball field!

Stuart Martin

From Rich Square, North Carolina, "Stu" Martin was a second baseman for Guilford College who went on to be a professional player. He was drafted by the St. Louis Cardinals in 1936 and was voted to the National League All Star team his rookie year. From 1936 to 1943 he played for the Pittsburgh Pirates, was traded to the Chicago Cubs and then went into the Navy for three years. In 1946 Stu played in the Pacific Coastal League and completed his career in the Coastal Plains League.

A Man Called "Block"

Charles "Block" Smith was undoubtedly one of the most be-loved coaches and teachers at Guilford College during his era. Not many other institutions or teams would have kept him as a coach for very long due to his record if it had not been for his heart. His record, when his two sports, basketball and football, are combined, is a staggering 6–109–3! Six wins in a six-year period across two sports. Because Guilford tolerated this record, as *Pride in the Past* says, "it is therefore important to look at Block Smith, the man."[6] From all accounts, his athletes and students enjoyed playing for him and having him as a teacher. They looked up to him as a man and as a great individual. It is amazing he was able to gain such devotion from his players that they felt sorry *for him* when they lost the game and not themselves![6] Having passed away in 1944, he was posthumously inducted into the Guilford College Sports Hall of Fame in 1971.[7]

Bob Jamieson

Robert "Bob" Jamieson was a student athlete at Guilford College that went on to become a famous local coach in Greensboro, North Carolina. While at Guilford he earned All Conference in two sports, football and basketball, but was a rare four-letterman at Guilford, which also included baseball and track. An interesting story of his athletic prowess: one time at Guilford the baseball game and track meet happened to be on the same day, at nearly the same time. Being on both teams, he managed to run and broad jump during half of the baseball innings, and then would go back to baseball to finish the innings.[8] An incredible athlete!

Bob Jamieson

After graduating in 1932, he coached at what is now called Grimsley High School.[11] Bob coached basketball, football, baseball, golf, swimming and track. Under his leadership, they won the state basketball championship three times, either won or tied the football state championship seven times, the golf state title four times, and won 14 Carolina AAU (Amateur Athletic Union) titles in swimming.[9] The stadium at Grimsley High today is named after him.[10]

Bob Jamieson has been inducted into five halls of fame: Guilford College, Guilford County, North Carolina Sports Hall of Fame, North Carolina High School Athletic Association, and the National High School Hall of Fame.[12] In addition, he helped found the North Carolina High School Coaching Clinic and the North Carolina Coaches Association. Guilford became later known as a "cradle of coaches," an unintentional but successful producer of coaches from its former athletes, a wonderful phenomenon I experienced during my era as well.[13]

ON TO GUILFORD COLLEGE!

I did not know all of the above history when I first came to Guilford, but while I was there, I came to know so much about it personally. When the 150th year anniversary of the college drew near in 1987, I was encouraged to write a book about the sports history of the college from its infancy. It was entitled *Pride in the Past*, which was published in 1987. It not only chronicled the past, from the college's humble beginnings, but brought it to the present as of 1986. The book was to be sold to anyone with the proceeds going to the Quaker Club.

However I am getting ahead of myself. Let us go back to Chowan College in the year 1955, when we just finished an 8–1 season with our best football team to date . . .

Edwin Brown

In 1955 I received a call from Ed Brown, chairman of the Board of Trustees at Guilford College in Greensboro, North Carolina. He was a former trustee at Chowan and knew what I had done for the college. During his phone call, he said the timing was right for me to come work for them at Guilford. "We want you go to Guilford College."

I remember my immediate answer, "Mr. Brown, I just built my new home!"

"Don't worry, I'll buy your house," he replied.

As it turned out, Mr. Brown lived up to his promise — he bought my house, and I moved to Guilford College in 1956. I was the new athletics director, head coach in football as well as a full professor in education and physical education. The other professors did not like me at first, as I came in making more than some of them.

Ernestine Milner, the president's wife made me very nervous. She was called the "Queen," with a bachelor's degree. During Commencement, I was told by Charlie Hendricks, who was in charge of Commencement, that I was to be ahead of her in the faculty line, because I had a Master's degree! I wanted no part of it, for fear of offending her since I was a new professor to her school. After much encouraging by Charlie I went to the head of the faculty line with the rest of the full professors with nothing said by Mrs. Milner.

After Mr. Brown called to tell me to come to Guilford College, I asked some of my men who played for me on the Chowan 1955 football team if they would play for me at Guilford and complete their education, since it was a four-year school and Chowan was a two-year school. Some of the men who came were: Herman Clark, quarterback, All America; Ben Rich, center and linebacker, All State, All America; Albert Vaughn and Jack Crenshaw, All State, All America; Jim Gravely All State and All America. All of these men came to Guilford College with me, in addition to Marty Domokus and Don Deaton, a halfback from Virginia. Darrell Allen, a sophomore from Ahoskie, North Carolina, gave us depth at center and Jim Gravely also came but did not play.[14] These were great men and I was excited to have them come with me to be on my teams at a new college and coaching opportunity, and I had hopes of accomplishing great things at Guilford in athletics.

Nereus "Nee" English

Guilford Trustee Nereus "Nee" English, along with Trustee Edwin Brown, helped me get to Guilford from Chowan College. So I felt a deep sense of appreciation to them for that, and for all their efforts at Guilford. When I came in 1956, Mr. English promised he would build a dormitory just to house the new athletes I would recruit for the teams. He did, that very same year.

Mr. English was a special man who was generous in his desire to help people who were in need of financial aid. As a trustee at Guilford he donated large sums of money to the college to help others financially. He played football and baseball at Guilford College, and after graduation he had ownership of several knitting mills in Thomasville, North Carolina, and an interest in the English Motor Company. He had an office in the Empire State Building in New York and was a very wealthy man who contributed to many civic groups. Nereus English's wife had a terminal illness that caused her to be in a wheelchair. He looked after his wife as long as she lived. He also sponsored our annual athletic banquets.

The Nereus English Athletic Leadership Award, named in his honor, continues to this day and is the school's highest honor for student athletes who reach the highest ideals of athletic accomplishment, leadership and academic achievement. I was asked to speak a few years ago at the English Award banquet. One student, after receiving the award, came up to me after I had told the story of Nereus English and his life during my speech. The student informed me he was glad to know Nereus English's story, because all he knew was that the school had given him an English award, and, knowing how his writing skills were, knew there had to be a mistake!

I remember once attending a conference in Florida. I was worried about the cost, which was $100, and I knew I would have to find some way to cover the expense when I returned home. I went to the post office to check my mail. I had a letter from Mr. English and was shocked when I opened the letter and found a check for $100. This kindness was typical of the man.

Dr. Clyde Milner was a wonderful president for Guilford College, a gentleman and a scholar. He was president at Guilford from the 1930s to the 1960s, and his presence and leadership on campus were felt everywhere. He believed in the power of academics, yet he believed that athletics and good sportsmanship were important to an institution. He believed in achieving, as the Guilford College newspaper once said, "moral victories" rather

Ernestine and Clyde Milner

than scoring victories at any cost.[15] This meant the focus was on playing honorably and with good sportsmanship, even if one lost the game. While I greatly respected Dr. Milner's position on the issue, I did however want to win. While I believed in developing men and women of character more than mere winners of games, going out onto the field *without* a desire to win and succeed was foreign to me. While I did not believe in winning at any cost (i.e., being dishonest), I also did not believe in letting the other team win, as Dr. Milner believed we should at times. All my career, I tried to inspire my students and athletes to become someone of worth and value, to instill good qualities in them and help them aspire to good character, integrity and moral values but also win!

An interesting story will give one an idea of the Guilford president. One day early in my coaching career at Guilford, the Green Bay Packers needed a local place to practice and warm up for an annual exhibition game in Winston-Salem. We invited them to practice on Guilford's football field. I just stood there on the sidelines after a Quaker practice, enthralled at the Green Bay team and how well they practiced football. They were professionals, without a doubt. While I was standing there in my coaching clothes, Dr. Milner came up behind me and watched with me for a few minutes quietly, just admiring the team's action. Seeing the "G" on the Green Bay helmets, characteristic of the Guilford "G," when he turned to leave he said to me, "My good man, I believe we are going to have a pretty good ball club this year." No one had told him that the Green Bay Packers were going to be practicing on our field that day!

Stuart "Rock" Maynard

When I came to Guilford College in 1956, I was going to be replacing Stuart Maynard as the athletics director and head football coach. Stuart was nothing but gracious as we worked together for 28 years.

Stuart Maynard originally played for Guilford College and was captain of the baseball and football teams at the college. In 1942 he was named the Best Senior Athlete. After a stint in the Navy, Maynard began coaching at Williamston, North Carolina, where he won the state football title in 1951. Another Guilford trustee, Elton Warrick of Goldsboro, was Stuart's mentor, and he wanted the best coaches at Guilford. Stuart returned to Guilford in 1952 where he served as athletics director, head football coach, director of phys-

Stuart Maynard

ical education and most notably head baseball coach where he received the nickname "Rock."[16]

Coach Maynard became the winningest Quaker baseball coach of all time and was named the 1966 NAIA Coach of the Year, as well as the Carolinas Conference Coach of the Year and he won four District 26 Coach of the Year honors. He coached at Guilford for 33 years, from 1951 to 1984. His coaching philosophy was a combination of teaching a solid foundation of the fundamentals of the game and keeping his teams in top physical condition, in which he also participated along with his players. He believed in teaching young boys to behave like men, stay fit and play so as to enjoy the game, but give it all you have.[17]

"Rock" had a crushing handshake and delighted in "taking down" his fellow handshaker. One Sunday at New Garden Friends Meeting before his passing he said to me, "Hey Herb, you must be working at it — you almost got the best of me!"

At his memorial service in 2013, the Guilford College baseball team stood on either side of the walkway to New Garden Friends Meeting, dressed in their uniforms, as they were going to play a game later that day. What a tribute it was for the winningest Quaker baseball coach. Guilford College dedicated the Maynard Batting Center in 2010 and installed "Rock's Rock" to honor the coaching great. Team players touch the rock for good luck before entering the stadium for a game.[16]

Stuart "Rock" Maynard

Claudette Weston

When I started my career at Guilford College in 1956 I had no idea my student secretary, Claudette Weston, would be so important to me. She became a source of information that helped me during a hard time at the college. I was the new athletics director as well as football coach and a full professor at Guilford. We had many obstacles to our program. Our athletic program was one that competed against strong schools such as Lenoir-Rhyne, Catawba,

Claudette Weston

Elon and Atlantic Christian (in Wilson, North Carolina) as well as East Carolina, Appalachian State and Western Carolina. We competed against teams that had scholarships at a time when our program did not. Claudette's ability to handle any problem, and in many instances without telling me about many of the problems, helped me through the early years.

Over the many years since that time, Claudette has stayed in touch with me, always with words of encouragement and support. As a legend, she helped me keep the program alive during a hard time. For that and much more, I am grateful.

Let's look at her accomplishments through the years, for there have been many since she graduated from Guilford. She has so many awards it is unbelievable. A few of them include the recent "7 Over Seventy Award," the Duke Energy Citizenship and Service award, and the Winston-Salem Foundation award. She even has the Joel A. and Claudette B. Weston award named for her and her late husband by the United Way Foundation. She has served on more than 50 boards, volunteering her time and energy. In 2013, Claudette was inducted for meritorious service into the Winston-Salem State University's Sport Hall of Fame.[18]

Claudette is passionate about children, which is seen in her involvement with Youth in Transition, an organization dedicated to helping children that have aged out of foster care. On a personal note, she has four children and eight grandchildren of her own.

To quote Claudette, upon receiving the most recent "7 Over Seventy Award", "I am flattered . . . . I am 80 years old and getting an award, that is pretty doggone good."[18]

First All America: John Meroney

I made "Yankee Stadium" in Cox Hall my headquarters as I began recruiting in 1956. One day Coach Martin, an assistant coach at the University of Virginia, called me about a super player at Bullis Prep, where Martin had previously coached. When I was at Chowan coaching the 1955 football team, Bullis Prep under Martin was the only school we could not beat that year. Coach Martin spoke with me about John Meroney, who was an exceptional halfback — fast, tough and an all-around great prospect. He told me Meroney's grades would not get him into Virginia. "We don't want another ACC school to get him. If you get him, you will have an All America." Upon his suggestion I went to meet John and invited him to campus.

The Virginia coach knew his talent and Johnny Meroney won our best tackler award 4 years in a row, became our first All America and also an outstanding sprinter on the track team. He also became team captain. An example of Meroney's ability: when he came to Guilford we opened up with Elon and I moved him to full back from half back. On the first play John ran 96 yards for a touchdown. On his second play, he ran 98 yards for a touchdown. On his third carry, he went 97 yards for a third touchdown.[19]

Meroney repeated the three touchdowns against conference leader Lenoir-Rhyne, the NAIA national champs. Not only could

John Meroney

he run, he was the best defensive player on our team for four years in a row. Chronicling this, *Pride in the Past* states, "It was one of the finest individual performances of the year." Dr. J. Floyd ("Pete") Moore, one of Guilford's memorable professors, who was always a strong supporter of athletics, asked John in religion class on Monday following the game: "Meroney, what was it like as you took the kick-off, started toward mid-field, cut back toward the middle, told Neil Jones to cut right and get the last defender, as you ran the entire distance for the touchdown?"

John, meaning no disrespect, but with his quick wit and sense of humor, replied: "Dr. Moore, it was a little like Moses must have felt when he reached the Red Sea and the waters parted at just the right time and he went right up the middle!"[19]

John Meroney was a good student, but the school president's wife, Ernestine, "The Queen," thought he came to Guilford College to only play football and let everyone know of her displeasure. Meroney fooled everyone and became a campus leader. When John Meroney graduated, Mrs. Milner told everyone she could how much she had changed her opinion of him. Meroney was not only a great athlete but a leader on campus with honors when he graduated. John had his four years as an exceptional athlete honored by the student body.

I felt later in life that John Meroney was the football player that had the greatest influence on me in all of my years of coaching. I appreciate the many memories that I have had with John. He helped with scouting reports and anything else to help us win. Meroney has left a legacy that will be hard to top. As an All America player, Meroney had a positive effect on the recruits and was invaluable to me throughout his career. The memories of John Meroney and his legacy will live on forever in the lives of others including mine. He had his jersey retired and it is on display in the trophy case in Ragan-Brown Field House at Guilford College for all to see, and he was also inducted into the Guilford College Hall of Fame.

Jim Stutts

One of the most outstanding athletes to wear the Guilford crimson and gray is Jim Stutts. Jim came out of military service as an older athlete who had a tremendous influence on his many team members. As a great catcher, he led the Quakers to its best seasons in the college's history. His leadership was powerful and influenced all of his teammates. He also held an old yet unusual record of being hit by pitchers that set a record in the nation! There are two schools of thought on the issue as to why he earned that record: one is that he stood too close to home and thus was hit more often, and the other is that the pitchers knew to aim for him because he was a good batter. We leave it up to the reader to decide which it was.

Besides being captain of the baseball team, Jim was captain of the football team. Jim played defensive end and was the best in the conference. Jim was also All America in baseball and football — quite an honor for two All America's to be bestowed on one player.

I really liked Jim Stutts for his leadership, especially as he helped the younger players. Coach "Rock" Maynard said that he relied on Jim Stutts to help work with the younger players as well. In all of his 33 years at Guilford College, Maynard praised Jim as the finest player and leader he had ever had to lead his teams. A high honor and compliment coming from a celebrated coach!

Very seldom do you find a man who has the ability to help the younger players on a team as Jim Stutts did for Guilford College. During his time at Guilford College, Jim led the Quakers by example with the positive influence he had on the younger players. His time in the military gave him outstanding leadership qualities. I admired Jim: he was a man who had not only the ability but the qualities to lead. I praised my tight end in football as the most successful player I ever coached.

As captain, Stutts worked tirelessly with the younger players who were freshman and needed extra coaching. Between Jim Stutts and John Meroney, Guilford had great players and men with character. With both Stutts and John Meroney, Guilford College was at its best in athletics in my years of coaching. These two men were Guilford College men of character.

Bob Smith

Every so often, an athlete goes beyond what they are expected to achieve with an extraordinary accomplishment, all without seeking praise for his effort. Bob Smith, a student-athlete from Virginia, was such a person. Bob was a hard-working student who was a backup fullback on the football team. As hard as he tried, he could not crack the starting lineup.

During the 1958 season Bob had an appendix attack and when he was rushed to the hospital he asked his doctor to make a small incision so it would heal sooner and get him back to practice. According to his doctor, he healed so quickly he returned to his teammates in record time. Now that is called dedication to your teammates and football!

Bob displayed unusual leadership in the locker room. However, he went the extra mile during spring football practice. Bob suffered a broken jaw and had it wired shut. No one could believe it when he put a face mask on and came in full pads the following day! Needless to say, I admired his desire to participate in the scrimmage but refused to let him play. Bob raised the bar high and was an unsung hero on the Guilford team.[21]

James "Muggers" Simpson

It was the final game of the year in 1958, and our Guilford team was looking forward to it being the last game. I was athletics director at that time, as well as football coach and track coach. So we all wanted it to be a good one and go out with a bang. We traveled up the mountain to Western Carolina University (WCU) in Cullowhee, North Carolina. WCU's record was 8–1, and ours was 3–6. At that time, Guilford College did not have scholarships for their athletic program, so that record was good for not having any scholarships.

The WCU head coach, Dan Robinson, and I were good friends, so he let our team come up a day early and spend the night in their field house. Our team was sound asleep in their triple decker bunk beds in the field house on the night before the game, when the WCU coach walked into the bedroom and called out, "Is there a Muggers Simpson here?"

All heads popped up at the sound, and one man replied that he was Muggers. His full name was James Simpson, but everyone called him Muggers. Mugger's wife, it turns out, was in labor. He said he would travel down the mountain, see his wife and make it back in time for our game the next day. Even though our coaches tried to discourage our third string halfback from going, Muggers said he could come back in time.

Coach Robinson told us that he would drive Muggers to Asheville to get a bus to Greensboro. Muggers told us goodbye, and that he'd be back soon. We all wished him and his wife the best. They then left for Asheville and the bus station. Muggers waited and waited. Unfortunately, no bus came, as they had unknowingly missed the last bus. Since Coach Robinson had already left for Cullowhee, Muggers hitchhiked the 240 miles to Greensboro, getting to the hospital at 4:00 am.

We got a call that morning from Muggers, to tell us that his wife had had a little boy. When our team heard the news, they had a team meeting that morning and agreed to win this game for "Little Muggers," his newborn son. Muggers was a really good guy, and very popular on the team. So to dedicate the game to Little Muggers was a testimony of their respect for him and how much everyone liked him.

Later, we were getting dressed for the game when the door opened and in walked our team doctor with Muggers! We were astounded to see him back, as we did not expect him to return after the birth of his son. The team gathered around Muggers, listening to the astonishing story of how he had hitchhiked to Greensboro all night long and got to see his son in the hospital nursery. Right after that, he called the team doctor, who was still in Greensboro at Guilford, and drove to get him from the hospital. Muggers had turned right around after seeing his son and

"Muggers" Simpson

came all the way back up the mountain, a four-hour trip with the team doctor to play in the final game. We all congratulated him on his new son and being a father. He did not tell us on the phone he was coming, so it was quite a surprise to see him in the locker room. Since he was going to play in the game, we went around the locker room, collecting Muggers' equipment that we had given to other players who needed it.

The excitement increased when I started Muggers at halfback that game on the receiving team. He took the ball and ran it back to mid-field on the first play of the game. In a tremendous game, Muggers ran wild. Inspired by his energy (even though he had traveled all night and barely slept), we upset a strong WCU team and had a great win.

What a locker room celebration we had! The players were hugging each other and cheering, especially Muggers. They all clapped Muggers on the back, congratulating him on having the greatest day of his life — winning the final football game as the underdogs and being a new father with a son. What a day that was! That was a happy bunch of guys on the ride down the mountain.

:::::

To my disappointment, in a poor act of sportsmanship, the students at WCU hanged Coach Dan Robinson in effigy after the game. They had been defeated by a team that had a worse record than they in the final game of the year, and the students were very unhappy. They did not believe in him much after that game.

What happened to Muggers and his new son, one may ask? Mugger's son grew up to be just like his dad. He became a college football player too, not a halfback but quarterback at Virginia Tech. The story of Muggers was told to future football teams who were also facing overwhelming odds as a testament to what one man's motivation can do. He became a legend at Guilford.[20]

Harold James, the "Kangaroo Kid"

A coach at Virginia Beach, Virginia, Fred Isaacs, called me and I could tell he was highly agitated. "Herb, I coached Harold James, a super athlete who suffered from polio as a child. He is one of the best all-around athletes I have ever coached. Harold is a super quarterback, basketball player and a great track star — a broad jumper, triple jumper and high jumper. Every time I send him to a university or college in Virginia, they ask him to take his sweat pants off, ask him to show them what he's got, what he can do with a withered leg. As soon as they see him they don't want him anymore. They don't even let him try out, they lose interest in him and do not offer him a scholarship. I recently remembered you were a good coach and athletics director who gives everyone a chance. I'll send Harold to you at Guilford College for a tryout — allow him to try out and you decide if you can use him in track and field and football."

Harold James

I said, "Sure!" I thought to myself, "What do I have to lose?"

Once Harold arrived, I wanted to see him high jump, so I asked him to take his sweat pants off and start jumping at six feet. This was easy for Harold. After a warm up, he easily cleared the bar. It was obvious — Harold was an athlete. I knew right away he would win for me and I had not even seen him tackle or throw a pass.

Harold starred in football as a defensive halfback. He had the knack for sensing plays and hit like a ton of bricks. In our opening game upset of our heavily favored rival, he played as we had never seen him play. It was in this game that he hurdled over an opposing blocker to make a vicious tackle. The surprised blocker looked up in bewilderment and shouted, "Hey you, are you some kind of a kangaroo?" The name stuck and his teammates affectionately referred to him as the "Kangaroo Kid." [22, 23]

During his four years at Guilford, Harold broke several existing records of both the school and the district. He scored more points in a dual meet and for an entire season than anyone before him at Guilford. In one meet, when the squad was limited in numbers, he ran the high hurdles, high jumped, broad jumped, pole vaulted, and threw the javelin and discus.

Harold came back after two narrow misses to try for the final jump in the conference track meet. The tension was terrific as he walked to the bar time and time again to get ready for the most important jump of his career. I prayed that he could make the height and win in his last meet of the year. I visualized the hours of work, the sacrifice and self-denial that this young athlete had put in and decided that win or lose he had been truly great. I could barely see as the crowd closed in on the pit for the last jump. Suddenly a tremendous roar was heard and I knew he had made the jump and was the new conference champion. People left the track in disbelief at this young man with the withered leg who refused to believe he could lose.[23]

We were once in a tight track meet when the last event found us in a tie — right before the final event, we needed a first place javelin throw to win. Harold came up to me and smiled and said, "Coach, we will win I promise you." With a tremendous throw, he threw his last javelin throw — his best ever — for our win.[22]

In football, Harold, during his senior year, was a legendary quarterback. Even the limp leg due to polio didn't stop him. With Harold at the helm at QB, Guilford College prospered for a great year. Coach Fred Isaacs was one of the happiest coaches anywhere as the "Kangaroo Kid" prospered and proved his recommendation of Harold James to be right.

During one football game an overly aggressive defensive lineman twisted Harold's little leg during a pileup, and as he limped off the field I saw a grin on his face. "Coach, don't get upset," he said. "I'm flattered that anyone would think that much of my ability." He climaxed a great personal year by being named to the All Conference team as a quarterback.

Later a writer interviewed him and asked him to tell of his greatest thrill in sports. "Was it the day you scored against the national champions? Was it the day you broke the district high jump record, won the conference high jump championship, the all conference football selection, or the honor of being chosen Virginia's 'Sportsman of the Year'?" He was quick to answer and his answer surprised me. He said, "None of these. It was the time when we played East Carolina when my coach [me!] put his arm around me before the game and told me he had decided that I was his number-one quarterback. For you see," he told the surprised writer, "I knew that in America, a handicapped boy could reach his goal if he wanted to badly enough."[23]

My experience with Harold James opened my eyes to the realization that many individuals with disabilities achieve success in sports without attention or fanfare. To these people the important thing is participation.[23] John E. Bignall, a wheelchair athlete, observed that physicians along with physical therapists find that sports participation is "an invaluable therapeutic tool." He also mentions how sport increases the person's feeling of self-worth and self-confidence so essential in the rehabilitation process.[22]

In 1983 I published one of the early texts dealing with athletes with disabilities, *The Right To Participate*.[22] This book was written before the historic Americans with Disabilities Act of 1990, and dealt with changing laws up to that point for participating athletes. I included the story of Harold James to illustrate how desperately people with disabilities desire to participate, and how if given the chance, they can triumph. For them, whether they win or lose, just the chance to participate is worth it all. Harold James, however, had the capability to win.

GOODWILL TOUR: A SUBSTITUTION

In May 1964, I received a telephone call from the AAU (Amateur Athletic Union) in New York, calling to invite me to take a six-man track and field team to Egypt and other countries on a goodwill tour. The AAU and the U.S. State Department had a tradition of their best athletes competing against the best teams from other countries around the world, as a way of promoting goodwill and unity with other countries through sport.

At that time I was completing my doctorate at Duke University. I was in my final Latin class at UNC Chapel Hill because Duke did not offer the course. My Latin professor said I could not miss my classes. Since I was so close to completing my doctorate and the professor would not let me make up any of my classes, I decided not to go on the AAU tour, even though it was a big honor to be asked to go. I was disappointed and asked my Guilford football and track coach John Stewart, who agreed to take my place on the tour to Africa and Egypt.

John came back and reported that he had had trouble on that trip, yet had learned some valuable lessons. "In case you ever go on a trip in the future," he said, "you need to remember some things." He went on to list some of those things, such as hiding one's money in their hotel room as theirs had been robbed, taking the passports of the athletes since some left without telling the coaches, remembering the first priority was to stay safe and come home if necessary, and trying *not* to win so as to keep international relations between the United States and the host nations to which they were trying to show goodwill. I kept those lessons in the back of my mind, in case I was ever allowed the opportunity to lead a Goodwill Tour.

THE FAR EAST: A GOODWILL TOUR

A year later in 1965, I received a call from the AAU, who again invited me to lead an eight-week goodwill tour with Coach Ron Richards, a track coach from California. Our Far East trip would go to Bangkok, Thailand, the Philippines, Singapore, Malaysia, and Hong Kong as well as Baguio City. This time, I was able to go.

We had an great team composed of all-star athletes, many just a step below Olympic level. We had seven athletes, men like

Norman Tate, an Olympic class sprinter and long jumper; Tom Ferrell, an 880-meter runner from St. John's; Rick Cunningham, our miler; and Andy McCrae, our hurdler from NC Central. The athletes had been selected and hand-picked by the AAU and the U.S. State Department from around the country to represent the United States in the Far East in track and field.[24] Dr. Leroy Walker, who later became the first African American president of the U.S. Olympics, had an outstanding track team at N.C. Central, where he served as coach.[25] Since I was involved with the AAU in track and field, we had gotten to know each other and became good friends. He coached many who later went to the Olympics, including our sprinter and long jumper Norman Tate. So I was confident we would do well.

Our team was excited about the trip and blended well as a team. Our team left from Newark Airport and flew to Los Angeles where we left for Vietnam. When we arrived at the airport in Seoul, South Korea, we learned the airport where we were originally supposed to land had been burned by the Vietnamese as the Vietnam War was going on.

The big test came when the U.S. team landed in Bangkok, Thailand. We were invited to attend their national meet at the Thai Stadium. We saw 57 members that would compete against our seven men the following day. When we competed against the Thai team, our men won every event.

Pole Vaulting

During one event my pole vaulter came up to me before his event and said, "Coach, I don't think I can do it." I asked him why. He informed me the ground was packed sand, and he would hurt himself on the landing. I told him, "Well, try at least two times."

On his first jump he came down and gashed his arm wide open. I took him to a doctor to have his arm sutured. While we were waiting for the doctor to come in, I was informed that the doctor had cerebral palsy that caused his hands to shake badly. My pole vaulter was very hesitant to have the doctor suture his arm. I assured him, saying it would be alright. Sure enough, the doctor came in with his hands shaking badly. But the doctor took the needle and thread in his capable hands and sewed him up beautifully.

Afterwards, my pole vaulter asked me, "How did you know?" I told him that I had just finished reading a book on a doctor who had cerebral palsy before we got on the plane, and knew that the doctor could do it. He trusted me after that.

Jegar and Norman Tate

One special event that took place in Hong Kong was the 100 meter dash. The Malaysians had a really fast runner named Jegathesan, who we called Jegar. He was projected to win. We had a runner named Norman Tate, who was the fastest man on our team. At 6´3˝ and 220 pounds, Tate was a physical specimen, all muscle and fit to run and long jump and triple jump. Norman worked hard for Dr. Leroy Walker, an Olympic coach who worked with Tate during his time at North Carolina Central.[25] So everyone was looking forward to the race.

Jegar ran in his first event (not against Tate), and won, but he did something unusual. As he crossed the finish line, he took the tape and broke it with his fingers instead of his chest, showing how far ahead he was of the other runners and how easily he had won. When he saw that, Tate turned to me and said, "Coach, when I beat him, I'm going to break the tape with my fingers." I told him, "Oh no, please don't do that. This is a goodwill tour, we don't want to make any enemies here. Just break the tape with your chest and that will be enough."

A huge crowd had gathered to see the race between Tate and Jegar. Tension was thick as they lined up for the long-awaited race. The race was close but Tate won, breaking the finish line tape with his fingers when he crossed as promised.

The supporters of Jegar were crushed but something happened that no one expected. Our team spontaneously jumped

Jegar (left) and Norman Tate (right), at the finish line

up, ran over and hugged *Jegar*! They were cheering him, telling him that no one had ever given Tate a race like that. He was a great runner, they said, for coming in second to a world-class athlete like Tate. The Malaysian team was very impressed by our genuine camaraderie and sportsmanship.

The next day, the press pointed out our story, saying that it was a fine example of sportsmanship and unity from another country. We got more positive press from that one incident than what we did the whole rest of the tour. The newspapers, radio and TV kept on praising the good sportsmanship on the part of Team USA. That one race paved the way for the rest of our tour in the Far East, because the other countries heard the story and knew that we truly were there to promote goodwill.

Off to Hong Kong

In Hong Kong, our team was given time off to rest. The officials needed one athlete to work in Hong Kong for the week — Ray

Saddler volunteered to go and work with the groups. One night Ray came back and told Coach Richards and me about the closing ceremonies with the groups of athletes he supervised. He was emotional when he told us that the teams gave him gift after gift and treated him so well. It was apparent that the teams loved Ray Saddler and his ability to help the group was a success.

Ray Saddler with schoolgirl in Hong Kong

Hong Kong was a good time for a break and our group was then ready to go to the Philippines and Bataan, especially Bataan where the Japanese during WWII had captured some of our soldiers and made them endure a long forced march. The infamous Bataan March, we learned, was brutal — the men were not allowed to have water and when one soldier bent down to drink water from a fountain, a Japanese soldier cut his head off. The men were placed in a prison camp across from a church. Later, our troops on General MacArthur's ship came to rescue the American prisoners. They defeated the Japanese and set the Americans free. The Americans rejoiced over their freedom and marched back toward Manila.

We had a good tour that became an interesting trip when our men were robbed in our Jeeps in Baguio City, Philippines. How they managed to do that while we were driving on the crowded streets I do not know but they did and ran off with their wallets. My men wanted to go after the pickpockets and search their homes but I told them to stop since we were on a goodwill tour. Our guide located the men who stole our money. Thankfully, they gave them the wallets and all was well.

One thing that was encouraging that happened was I had many Asian athletes come up to me after events and ask me how they, being so small of stature, could reasonably expect to compete and win against bigger, stronger athletes from places like the United States or Europe? This was, at first, a hard question for me to answer, and at first I did not have a good answer.[22]

The more I thought about it and had this question asked of me, I remembered the story of Harold James, the "Kangaroo Kid", who had one leg that was smaller than the other due to polio. However he was an incredible athlete, track star and football quarterback. In the face of tremendous odds he was able to withstand and triumph. I began to relate this story to the different athletes that asked me of their chances of competing internationally. The story of Harold James really encouraged them, and

Norman Tate "in flight" at the high jump

reminded them that it is not always size or strength that wins the day, but ability and heart.[22]

A sad thing happened when we returned from our Goodwill trip to the Far East in 1965. I visited Mr. English, my good friend and a Guilford trustee, in the hospital the same day our plane landed. As I got ready to leave his room, I gave him a carved wooden Madonna that I had bought in the Philippines.

While on the goodwill tour, our group went to a mountain top where the village was very poor. The people had made beautiful carvings out of wood and were selling them. Our men refused to buy them for the extremely low prices they were selling to us of ten cents and twenty cents apiece, because we felt it was not enough money. Our men bought them for one and two dollars apiece instead. I bought two carvings of the Madonna that were beautiful. When I visited Nereus English in the hospital after our trip I gave him one. He loved the beautifully carved piece and said that he would put it on the shelf behind him to protect him through the night. He said, "I'll put it behind me to watch over me."

The next morning I arrived at our gym to find a large crowd of students and faculty. One of them came over to me to tell me that Mr. English had died that night, right after I left the hospital. I found out that a blood clot went to his heart and killed him.

At Chapel later that day, the football coach, baseball coach and basketball coach stood up and each dedicated the next year in athletics to Mr. English. "What followed is little short of a modern miracle that took place in three sports that season."[26]In football, we went 8–2, baseball 28–9, and basketball 16–6 and went to the national championship. All three sports had their best records ever. In Guilford's very first year of having grants-in-aid we set these astonishing records in all three sports — truly a "modern miracle." In large part this was due to the generous funding of Mr. English, who had allowed Guilford to finally receive grants-in-aid for their athletes.[26]

We would never have achieved so much in athletics without the generous help of Mr. English.

RESOURCES

1. *Pride in the Past*, pp. 1–3. Written by Herb Appenzeller. Published by Guilford College, 1987.
2. *Pride in the Past*, p. 15.
3. *Pride in the Past*, pp. 30–31.
4. *The New York Times* (1981), https://www.nytimes.com/1981/05/18/sports/baseball-s-perfect-12.html.
5. https://www.merriam-webster.com/dictionary/twirler, updated 29 July 2018.
6. *Pride in the Past*, pp. 59–63.
7. https://www.guilfordquakers.com/history/Profiles/Smith-_C?view=bio
8. *Pride in the Past*, pp. 42–43.

9. http://www.greensborosports.org/guilford-county-sports-hall-fame/robert-jamieson

10. https://www.guilfordquakers.com/history/Profiles/Jamieson-_R?view=bio

11. https://www.ncshof.org/bobjamieson

12. http://www.nfhs.org/resources/hall-of-fame/inductees-by-state/

13. *Pride in the Past*, pp. 88–92.

14. *Pride in the Past*, pp. 78.

15. *Pride in the Past*, p. 64.

16. www.guilfordquakers.com/sports/bsb/2012-13/releases/20130403dcimh5

17. *Pride in the Past*, pages 102, 196–197.

18. *SPARK Magazine*, published by the *Winston-Salem Journal*, Winston-Salem, NC. Mid-summer issue, 2017.

19. *Pride in the Past*, p. 81.

20. *Pride in the Past* by Herb Appenzeller, pp. 84–85.

21. *Pride in the Past*, pp. 92–93.

22. *The Right to Participate*, by Herb Appenzeller, p. 25 and passim.

23. *Pride in the Past*, pp. 91–92.

24. *Pride in the Past*, p. 123.

25. https://www.nytimes.com/2012/04/25/sports/olympics/leroy-t-walker-us-olympic-committees-first-black-president-is-dead-at-93.html.

26. *Pride in the Past*, p. 109.

CHAPTER 7

:: :: ::

When I arrived at Guilford College in 1956, the athletic program was at the bottom of the conference in all sports. The reason was a lack of athletic grants. The conference allowed 45 football grants, and Guilford had none. As a result, the men and women played hard, but rarely achieved success. There was little chance of winning conference contests at this time.

In 1962, the trustees of Guilford College called an important meeting to drop all athletics in favor of intramurals. When they announced that that was their agenda, I was shocked, but knew something had to be done to save the athletic program. I immediately asked where was Dr. Purdom, the department chair for athletics. "He is teaching class and is not to be disturbed," was their reply.

Realizing that they would not listen to my efforts to keep athletics, I decided something drastic had to be done, something unheard of. I ran over to the physics building to find Dr. Purdom. He was there just as they said, teaching class. When he saw me, he knew something was wrong. Dr. Purdom stepped outside the classroom for a moment and I explained the situation to him. He immediately dismissed class and beat me back to the boardroom in a sprint, despite his seventy years of age![1] Due to his persuasive efforts, the Trustees initiated a committee to determine the impact that sports had had on Guilford.

The Trustee Committee later voted in favor of keeping athletics, and to allow scholarships for the athletic program. What a difference that made. It turned the program around, as the history books show. We went from being at the bottom of the conference in all sports to winning the National Championship in basketball only eleven years later! Dr. E.G. Purdom was the one who saved the Guilford College athletic program.[1]

THE PARKER FAMILY

There have been several families whose names have lasted for many years at Guilford College, with children and even grandchildren attending the same school. One of those was the Parker family, with a heritage starting in 1906 with the first Parker to attend Guilford College, Ruth Parker. Her son, George, and his

The Parker family 2019

wife, Elizabeth ("Lib"), graduated from Guilford, and later on became trustees. Their children became good athletes at Guilford, graduating at different times — Conrad '62, Elwood '64, Edgar '69, John '72, and Elizabeth Parker '76. Quite a family dynasty.

Three of the sons made All Conference — John, Elwood, and Edgar. Edgar was on the Guilford baseball team, one of the star pitchers who went to the championship. They did not win, but earned second place due to not catching a fly ball. Just going to the NAIA national championship however was a real honor![2]

Elizabeth Parker Haskins, their sister, was the second female to be inducted into Guilford College's Sport Hall of Fame (behind Coach Gayle Currie). The school has even retired Elizabeth's jersey. She made 42 points in one basketball game — the first female Guilford athlete to do so, which was a school record until 2005. Elizabeth became the MVP in 1976 and was voted Best Athlete. She won multiple awards at Guilford, including the Algie Newlin Senior History Award and was named to Who's Who Among College and University Students.[3] She went on to become a high school coach, and was later selected to be on the East-West All Star Basketball coaching staff.[2]

The Parkers were truly good, not only in athletics but in academics. The brothers, Elwood and Edgar, were advanced math teachers and became nationally known mathematics researchers. As the book *Pride in the Past* states, "The Parker family is truly remarkable for its love and dedication to Guilford College in academics, athletics, leadership and service to the teaching and coaching professions."[2]

GARY YORK

When Gary York came in 1961, Guilford College was only able to offer grants-in-aid to their athletes, not full athletic scholarships. Gary qualified for a grant, but it was not long before I had to take it away because Gary told his friends in Mount Airy that he had a full athletic scholarship to play football. This constituted a lie in my book. Later Gary proved that he could earn a grant to play for Guilford and I gave him his grant back.

Gary was a guard in football and without a football scholarship Gary made All Conference. Later, Gary was named captain of the team which was an honor he earned.

When Gary made the All Conference team at Guilford College, it was in a tough conference with schools like Catawba, Lenoir-Rhyne, Elon, Western Carolina, Appalachian and Atlantic Christian. All those schools had 45 full grants and Guilford had none. In time, Guilford defeated Elon, Appalachian, Emory and Henry, and Western Carolina. The Western Carolina's season record was 12–1 and a win for Guilford was the highlight as Western Carolina had a great offense. The Quakers shut them down and won a great victory. Stars for Guilford on that team were Jim Stutts, Gary York, Brodie Baker, Harold James, Ralph Nelson and Wayne Henley.

As Guilford football coach I believed this team was one of my best, led by John Meroney — the Quakers' very first All America in football and also All Conference and All District, as well as Wayne Henley, three time All America. Wayne Henley was a married student who was going to drop football because it was so tough on him. He was about to drop it until his wife told him not to quit. He stayed and worked himself into shape and made the All Conference and All District teams, along with the third team All America at tackle.

Gary earned both All Conference and All District for Guilford College as a guard. Quite an honor since the conference guards had talent, but despite a lack of scholarships he earned All Conference honors. He was joined by Ralph Nelson in earning the honors.

One night when Gary enjoyed himself too much at a basketball game at High Point, Mrs. Milner, the president's wife wanted to have his grant removed. I refused to take his grant away from him and gave him another chance, which he never forgot. He graduated from Guilford in 1965 and we kept up with each other. Gary wrote many, many letters over the years to me and in them he always said, "Thanks for see-ing some good in me."

Gary York

York went on in his life to become a Guilford trustee, a UNC-TV trustee, and the former owner of Neigh-bors Stores — which at one time was a 26-convenience store chain. He is also the owner and CEO of 100.9 WIFM radio in Mt. Airy, N.C., where he resides. His radio station has a call to action which is a reflection of his benevolent spirit, that reads: "Be generous to the community. Advocate worthy causes. Speak for those who need a voice."[4] His monthly newsletter which he has been sending out for 24 years, called "The Communicator," highlights community servants, some of whom would otherwise go unnoticed. He continues to run a local bed and breakfast called Dr. Flippin's, as well as the Vintage Rose Wedding Venue, both located in Mt. Airy, N.C.[5]

SETH MACON

I first met Seth through our mutual involvement with Jefferson Lake when I directed the summer swimming program there. Al-though we were both involved with Guilford at the time, we had not met until working for that program. He was a great guy.

There are many stories of Seth Macon, but this write-up on the Guilford website says it best:

> Seth C. Macon '40, one of Guilford's most dedicated alumni and ardent supporters, rose from humble beginnings on a farm in rural Randolph County to

a position of leadership with the College and in the Greensboro community.

When he died Feb. 17 at the age of 96, President Emeritus Bill Rogers, during whose tenure Seth became trustee chair, said, "We have lost one of the remaining giants of community responsibility, religious and social insight, and meaningful leadership."

President Jane K. Fernandes called it the end of "a 70-plus-year love affair" between Seth, his late wife Hazel Monsees Macon '41 Guilford graduate, and their alma mater.

Seth was born in 1919 about 20 miles south of Greensboro. World War I had just ended. A flu epidemic had killed more than 20 million people worldwide. Women were not yet eligible to vote. Movies were silent, and radio had just been invented.

His parents were Quakers, Oran Thomas "O.T." Macon and Kate Craven Macon, and he grew up in the Providence Friends Meeting. The family had ties to Guilford through Eli Macon, Seth's great-grandfather, who attended New Garden Boarding School in the 1800s.

Seth's half-brother Hershell and brother Leonard preceded him at Guilford. Leonard and Seth attended during the Great Depression. "Everybody knew what would be needed because the process had just been gone through with Leonard. He had paved the way for me," Seth wrote in his 2006 memoir, *Uphill Both Ways.*

Seth worked for a year after finishing high school and enrolled at Guilford in 1937. To help cover the cost of college, he took various jobs on campus as a maintenance man, coal shoveler, garbage collector

Hazel and Seth Macon

and boiler-room operator, all at 25 cents an hour. For spending money he cut hair in his room in Cox Hall (now Hege-Cox Hall).

Football coach Block Smith saw Seth hauling trash at the end of his sophomore year and recruited him to play despite a complete lack of football experience. Seth played for two years, starting every game at left guard as a senior and helping the team to a 6–3 record.

At Guilford he met Hazel, an outstanding student who was recruited from her Davidson County high school to the College by President Clyde Milner and Professor Garness Purdom. Seth and Hazel sat next to each other in compulsory chapel, as seating was assigned alphabetically.

"At first I walked behind her from chapel to our next classes at King Hall," Seth wrote in *Uphill Both*

Ways. "It wasn't long before I started walking with her ... I have frequently said, 'I didn't make very good grades at college but I got a great wife.'"

Seth took a job with Jefferson Standard Life Insurance Company after graduating and then served in the Army Air Corps Training Command for six years following the outbreak of World War II.

Seth's military service and first job with Jefferson Standard took the Macons to Tampa, Florida.; Ft. Worth, Texas; and Asheville, North Carolina, but they returned to Greensboro in 1946. He worked with Jefferson Standard for 44 years until his retirement as a senior vice president in 1984.

Hazel and Seth had two children, both of whom attended Guilford. Carol graduated in 1969; Randall in 1974.

Guilford called on Seth to serve on the presidential search committee that recommended hiring Grimsley Hobbs '47 in 1966. As an alumnus, parent and community leader, Seth was invited to become an associate trustee of the College in 1969 — only Quakers were allowed on the board and Seth had joined the Baptist denomination.

When the rules were changed later in 1969, Seth became a full-fledged trustee. He served on the presidential search committee that recommended hiring Bill Rogers in 1980 and became the first non-Quaker chair of the Board of Trustees the same year. He served as board chair for eight years and remained an active trustee until 1997.

Seth and Hazel were longtime President's Club members, supporting many College initiatives. For example, they established the Seth C. and Hazel M. Macon GOAL Student Loan Fund and the Seth and Hazel Macon Professorship. They made an estate gift to support the creation of a welcome center on campus.

The Alumni Association Board of Directors, of which Seth was once a member, presented him with its Distinguished Service Award in 1978. He was inducted into the Guilford College Athletics Hall of Fame in 2002.

In *Uphill Both Ways*, Seth expressed the gratitude he and Hazel felt for Guilford College "for the help we have received to prepare us for, and help us have, a good life, which is much, much more than just making a good living."[6]

BILLY ARMFIELD

Every once in a while someone comes along that is a modest person who makes a gift to the athletic program in a wonderful financial way to help the program. That someone was Billy Armfield.

I received a phone call one day, inviting me to his office after 5 o'clock to talk about our athletic program. Billy was the most

Herb Appenzeller field and scoreboard at Guilford College. The Armfield Family Foundation was so generous over the years and when they were asked they gave more money to update Armfield Athletic Center and asked that the field be named for me. Billy Armfield, a special friend of mine and Guilford College, is to be remembered.

generous donor I ever met. Besides helping fund our athletic facility, named for the Armfield family, Billy was always asking on our behalf, checking on the Armfield Athletic Center and parts of it that were funded by the Edward M. Armfield, Sr. Foundation.

When I first met with Billy I thought he was a Guilford man. He quickly told me Carolina was his school, but he would like to hear about the athletic program at Guilford. I was very embarrassed but very grateful that he took such an interest in Guilford Athletics.

Billy worked in the textile business, starting out at Madison Throwing Company, founding Macfield and subsequently merging with Unifi, Inc. Billy formed Spotswood Capital Investment LLC, a private investment company to carry out his charitable gifts.

One example of his kindness was when coach Charles "Charlie" Forbes had an 8–2 record, and I received a call from Billy asking if we would like to schedule a dance for the coaches and their spouses. I told him I would check with our coaches right away. In the meantime, Billy suggested another venue. He scheduled a trip to the Angus Barn in Raleigh in a reserved room for our coaches. We could eat whatever we wanted of the Angus steak and beverages also. The food was amazing. We were treated royally and given bottles of wine and other beverages to take home. All this was funded by Billy himself. This was a highlight of our football season and one we have never forgotten during all my years as football coach and 37 years as athletics director.

Billy Armfield could always do anything for us, and his sudden death was a tragedy to all of our athletes and coaches at the college. He was a giver.

I have a letter from him that I call a "keeper," written by my special friend. The letter was written from the heart and one I will treasure as long as I live. May God bless Billy's family with His everlasting love and the knowledge that he was loved during his life. May I always remember Billy and all he has done. He was one in a million and loved by so many of us.

JERRY STEELE

Jerry was co-captain of Wake Forest's 1961 ACC Championship team, as well as being a two-time member of an ACC all-academic team and later was inducted into the Wake Forest and the NC Sports Halls of Fame. After completing his master's degree at the University of North Carolina, Steele took over a struggling basketball program at Guilford College in 1962. Prior to his being hired at Guilford College, the business manager David Parsons told President Milner that hiring Steele would bring "big-time basketball" to Guilford. I remember responding to that by saying, "Steele will be coaching basketball, *not playing it*." How prophetic David Parsons was in 1962.[7]

Jerry Steele

Surprisingly, Steele won the NAIA Coach of the Year for District 26 his first year coaching at Guilford. This award was given because, of Guilford's losses, many were only by a few points that season. The fact that Guilford could come so close to winning while being a non-scholarship school gave them a good reputation as a team who fought hard. Among those on the team were the 6′2″, All Conference player Dan Kuzma, who scored 45 points in one game. Lloyd Turlington, David Odom, Elwood Parker and Bill Shirley formed what we called the "men of Steele."[7]

In 1964, the basketball team was, in the words of player David Odom, in "a pathetic state at best."[7] In order to boost his team's and the school's morale, the season's scheduling was rearranged so that the non-scholarship schools were played multiple times but only once against the bigger teams such as Appalachian, Elon and Western Carolina. In spite of the other teams' protests,

Coach Jerry Steele (standing, far right), assistant coach Jack Jensen (standing, far left) and 1966 NAIA District 26 champions with star Bob Kauffman number 44 (standing)

the unusual scheduling policy worked! Although they did not win big that year either, the wins they were able to accomplish spurred the Quakers on to strive for greater heights. In the words of the book *Pride in the Past*, "The Quakers were for real and the campus was alive."[7]

Following a 5–21 record his first year, Steele throughout his years at Guilford led the Quakers to two conference titles, four district championships and made four appearances in the NAIA National Tournament in Kansas City. In 1969–70, Steele guided Guilford to 29 consecutive wins and a 32–5 record while finishing fourth in the nation. In 1970, Steele took a job as assistant coach with the American Basketball Association's Carolina Cougars, with Jack Jenson taking his place at Guilford as head Coach.[8]

Steele became head coach midway through the 1970 season with the Cougars. In 1972, Steele went on to become the head coach at High Point College.[10] In 31 seasons, Steele became the school's all-time winningest basketball coach with a record of 458–412.[9] His overall collegiate coaching record was 609–486.

Steele was inducted into the NAIA Hall of Fame, Guilford County Sports Hall of Fame, North Carolina Sports Hall of Fame, Guilford College Sports Hall of Fame and the Wake Forest Sports Hall of Fame. At High Point University, the Jerry and Kitty Steele Center is named for Jerry Steele and Kitty his wife.[9]

CHARLIE HARRISON

Charlie Harrison was a manager and athletic trainer at Guilford College of the men's basketball teams, working under coach Jerry Steele. Although he never attended Guilford, he became actively involved in life at Guilford, the student-athletes and the coaching staff. He so honored the staff and students that he drove athletes to games, made breakfast or dinners for them at his house, and attended numerous funerals and weddings.[11] A funny story shows his devotion to Guilford athletics: one night at an away game at Western Carolina University, he cheered until he was hoarse as the Quakers obtained the victory. That spring, the Quaker cheerleaders made him an "honorary cheerleader" at the Awards Convocation.[11]

Charlie Harrison went on to become a successful basketball coach at the college and professional level.[12] While attending Indiana University, he became a graduate assistant coach under Bobby Knight, whose team finished third in the 1974 NCAA Division I Men's Basketball Tournament. He was the assistant coach for Clemson University, the Buffalo Braves (NBA), and the University

Charlie Harrison

of Oklahoma, before becoming acting head coach at the University of New Mexico and assistant head coach at Iowa State University (1980–82). He later moved to East Carolina University (1982–87), taking over the head coaching position from Guilfordian and former athlete David Odom.[12]

After his coaching years, Charlie created an environmental services company called UTTS, which grew into a $3.5 million dollar company that he later sold. He now lives in Atlantic Beach, North Carolina. We have stayed in touch and stayed friends throughout the years. He has been inducted into the Guilford College Athletics Hall of Fame.[12]

DAN KUZMA

Dan Kuzma was an incredible player, playing under Jerry Steele, who scored over 1,500 points in his career at Guilford. He set multiple records in athletics, and later broke a few of his own; one of his records still stands today at Guilford (23 field goals in one basketball game). One of the top ten leading career scorers in Guilford history, his #22 jersey has been retired. His name is honored in the Guilford College Athletics Hall of Fame.[13]

DAVID ODOM

In high school David Odom was a "three-sport star" at Goldsboro.[14] After graduating in 1960, he went on to Guilford College. There he played great football and basketball from 1961–1965. From the book *Pride in the Past* comes an excerpt from David Odom himself on playing basketball at Guilford and reliving the memories of those days:

> Never in the annals of sport has so much been accomplished with so little. When Coach Jerry Steele took over, the basketball team was in a pathetic state at best. Four years later, respectability was a given and

even realistic expectations and future championships were a part of every Guilfordians conversation....

But mostly I can still feel the atmosphere in our dressing room after every game. I can smell the sweat of every win and loss. I can still hear Coach Steele pray as only he could; the thanks he gave for the opportunity to work at Guilford and coach us; he prayed for those less fortunate than we; and he prayed for our families.

In the early years were born the seeds of conference, district and NAIA championship. A few years later when Coach Jack Jensen and his players walked to center court in Kansas City to accept Guilford's championship trophy, Coach Jerry Steele, Coach Roy Williams, my teammates and I walked with them. The crowd could not see us, but make no mistake, we were there.[7]

It was this "special feeling" that David Odom mentioned that describes the heart of what *Legends from the Locker Room* is all about. It is that spirit of love in the locker room, the feeling for one's team and teammates that can bond a team together and can make them one — unified. The love, the camaraderie, the team spirit and loyalty for each other: that is

David Odom with Herb Appenzeller

David Odom

what defines a team and is the essence of what a true team is all about. It takes men and women of character to create this kind of bond for each other, and that is what David Odom's team had.

Guilford College has been called in times past the "cradle of coaches," meaning out of it came former athletes who became outstanding coaches.[15] Few other schools approached the ratio of athletes who went on to become coaches that Guilford had. Most of them became football coaches, although a few were basketball coaches. David Odom, for example, was one.

From there David went on to become a head coach in basketball for over 40 years. He coached at East Carolina University, the University of Virginia, and Wake Forest University where he coached for 12 years. Odom completed his coaching career at the University of South Carolina. His career record is 240 wins to 132 losses. David has been inducted into the North Carolina Sports Hall of Fame and the Guilford College Athletic Hall of Fame.[16, 17]

DANIEL "DANNY" C. SURFACE

Danny Surface was a special player, not only in his ability but in his character as well. His high school and college athletic career was illustrious. While at Blacksburg High in Virginia, Danny became a star in three sports, and all together obtained 10 letters in all three, which were baseball, basketball and football. Danny came to Guilford after completing two years of football and baseball at The College of William and Mary.[18] His coach was Marv Levy, prior to his becoming coach for the Buffalo Bills. Danny followed Bill Johnson, the defensive coordinator from William and Mary to Guilford.

While at Guilford, Danny earned many honors as an athlete. In football he played defensive back and running back on the 1965 team that went 8–2, which was the first winning football program we had had in 18 years.[19] He also earned the Best Hustler award in 1965 on the football team. He won the Richard Joyce Sportsmanship Award at Guilford two times. Danny also played baseball, where he played for three seasons, helping us earn an Area 7 title and go to the NAIA World Series in 1966, where we won fourth place.[19]

Academically, he completed his degree in Physical Education in 1967. After his years at Guilford, Danny went on to earn his Master's degree in Physical Education from the University of Tennessee. He went to Chowan as an associate professor and coach, where he stayed for a combined 37 years. He was the defensive coordinator to the coaching great Jim Garrison at Chowan, helping to coach players such as George Koontz, Mike Grant, and Robert Brown.[18]

He later became the Assistant Athletics director of Operations in

Danny Surface

1998, and was a Faculty Marshall at Chowan University. In 2005 he was inducted into the Guilford College Sports Hall of Fame, and then the Chowan University Hall of Fame in 2009.[18, 19] Sadly, he passed away in December of 2011, mourned by all who loved him at Chowan and Guilford.

TOMMY GRAYSON

Tom "Tommy" Grayson was a Rocky Mount, N.C., native who was a gifted athlete in baseball and football. I felt that Tommy needed prep work to be eligible for college, so I sent him to Chowan College. Tommy did well in his courses and great in football at Chowan where he earned All America. When Tommy came to Guilford College he earned All America honors as a halfback in

Tommy Grayson

football and third baseman in baseball. He also won All Conference and All District honors in football. He was at Guilford from 1965 to 1968. Tommy earned the NAIA All America honors in baseball, and he led the conference in rushing and scoring at Guilford in 1966.[20]

When the University of Massachusetts came south to play Guilford College, they made fun of the facilities. During the game, Tommy was our lead-off hitter. The pitcher from UMass threw and Tommy hit the ball and drilled it over the fence for a home run. They did not make fun of our team anymore after that! We won the game because of Tommy that day.

An unusual thing happened at Guilford while Tommy was there. Tommy took a class called Education 220 with me and passed with a "B." The following semester, he inadvertently took the same course again, thinking it was the next level Education course. The reason he was confused was because I used a different book to teach the same class, so he never recognized that he had taken the wrong class until the end of the year. Tommy was never upset about it, but just blamed himself for the mistake. I felt bad for that happening, but I also did not recognize that Tommy was retaking his class until too late. Sadly, the second time he got a "C" instead of a better grade.

Tommy Grayson played semi-pro baseball in Detroit for the AAA team. One step up and he would have been in the major leagues. Today, Eastern Guilford High School has named its football field for Tommy. He is a Hall of Fame recipient at Chowan College and Guilford College, as well as the Guilford County Sports Hall of Fame. [21] He occasionally coaches baseball at Guilford, his alma mater, to this day.

MARY GARBER

One of my favorite newspaper reporters was Mary Garber of the *Winston-Salem Journal*. In her early years of reporting she could not enter the locker room of the winning team or, as she preferred, the losing team, because she was a female. Mary's writing was outstanding and well written for the sports fan by its plain language and use of graphic and colorful language. It took years for Mary to be the first woman to enter a locker room for men on a local and national basis.

It took years for Mary to gain the acceptance by the press due to her gender. However, Mary later gained not only local atten-

New York Times

Mary Garber[29]

tion but also national recognition. Her long career began with humble status in 1946 due to discrimination against her gender and slowly grew to fame by the time she retired in 1997.

Mary was the recipient of many national honors. Mary was a trusted colleague and a modest, humble friend of sports accuracy and well-reported information. Mary always preferred to write about the losers rather than the winners. She is in the North Carolina Sports Hall of Fame as well as the National Sportscasters and Sportswriters Hall of Fame. She got her chance to be a sportswriter during WWII when the men went off to war, and then had to "earn" her seat when they came back in the all-male press box.[22] She was also the first woman to cover African American high school games as well, during a time of segregation.

Reporter Mary Garber, a pioneer for female journalists.

Mary died at age 92 with many honors and

awards for her writing and she certainly had the longest career. She and Winston-Salem State University's legendary coach Clarence "Big House" Gaines became close during Garber's coverage of WSSU Athletics. It was the efforts of Gaines and the writing of Garber that helped to put WSSU athletics into the national spotlight.[23]

For years Mary Garber was important to me for her friendship and cooperation on writing many stories with me. Her friendship led me to Wilt Browning, a sports writing legend who was an outstanding sports writer on every level of sports.

Mary told the story that when an African American male sportswriter joined her in the booth, she said to him, "Welcome, fellow minority." He laughed and laughed.[22]

BOB KAUFFMAN

Bob came to Guilford College to play basketball for coach Jerry Steele and was predicted to be the best basketball player in the country by major newspapers. Bob was unable to get into Wake Forest so Horace "Bones" McKinney recommended him to Coach Jerry Steele. What a fortunate recommendation that was!

Kauffman was one of those early basketball players that put Guilford College on the map, so to speak. His athletic ability and rise to stardom allowed others to hear about his deeds at a small North Carolina Quaker college, and helped us to gain fame through his efforts. With his ability to score points and win games, Guilford went to the NAIA national tournament, a feat which had never been done before in the history of the college. After he graduated in 1968, he was drafted by the Seattle Supersonics and his career took off. He played for the SuperSonics, the Chicago Bulls and the Buffalo Braves in the NBA.[24]

Here is a personal tribute to the star player, as published by long-time radio announcer and columnist David "Doc" Searls' blog:

When the Los Angeles Clippers open their first game at home this season 2015, I want them to pause and celebrate their original franchise player: Bob Kauffman, the team's all-star center for its first three seasons, when they were the Buffalo Braves.

In fact, I think the team should retire Bob's jersey, #44. For the ceremony the team should also bring out his four daughters, all of whom were also basketball stars: Lara and Joannah at Georgia Tech, Carey at Duke and Kate at Clayton State. Bob died on July 27, 2015 at age 69.

Bob was an amazing player to watch, a privilege I enjoyed often as a fellow student at Guilford College. Guilford was nowhere before Bob arrived and a powerhouse by the time he left. The same went for the Braves.

At 6′8″ and 240, Bob was a big guy, but he played bigger. Here's what Guilford wrote about him when he passed away:

Kauffman scored 2,570 points on 64 percent field-goal shooting and collected 1,801 rebounds in his 113-game career, all current school standards. He also holds Guilford marks for career scoring average (22.7 ppg.), single-game rebounds (32), single-season rebounds (698, 1967–68), career rebounding average (15.9), career field goals (943), single-season field goal percentage (.712, 1967–68), single-season free throws (273, 1966–67), career free throws (684) and single-season free-throw attempts (344, 1966–67).

Great stats, but none suggest how tough and intimidating Bob was as a player. I remember watching one Braves game against the Celtics on TV, pleased when the announcer said Bob was the only center in the NBA who knew how to play Boston's

Dave Cowens, straight up. Amazingly, I just found an account of what followed, in 30 Things About Dave Cowens:

. . . he slugged Guilford's Bob Kauffman, appropriately nicknamed "Horse," at the foul line, then patiently waited for Kauffman to swing back. Kauffman hit Cowens so hard Cowens finished the game wearing an eye patch.

And yet he was totally generous: a consummate team player. I remember Bob McAdoo's first game with the Braves, against the Knicks at Madison Square Garden. Bob grabbed an offensive board he could have put right back in; but instead he kicked it out to the rookie, so the kid could get off his first pro shot.

Bob's pro career started as what today we'd call a lottery pick: he was taken third in the 1968 draft by the Seattle Supersonics (now the Oklahoma City Thunder) behind future Hall-of-Famers Elvin Hayes and Wes Unseld. But the Sonics didn't know what to do with Bob. Nor did the Chicago Bulls, where he played the next year.

Then Bob got lucky. Thanks to various trades and player shufflings, he landed with the Buffalo Braves, an expansion team, for their inaugural season. The fit was perfect. Here's Jerry Sullivan in *The Buffalo News*:

In the Braves' first season of 1970–71, Kauffman averaged 20.4 points, 10.7 rebounds and 4.5 assists. He averaged 18.9 points and 10.2 rebounds in '71–72 and 17.5 points and 11.1 rebounds in '72–73. He made the Eastern all-stars in all three seasons for Buffalo teams that lost 60 games.

As his daughter Lara put it to Jerry, [Steele], Bob left his heart in Buffalo:

"The Buffalo fans from all over, people who moved to Atlanta or wherever I go, they all remember my dad," Lara Kauffman said. "What people remembered about my dad was he played very blue-collar. I think he was sort of a reflection of a lot of people in the Buffalo community the way he played. He wouldn't back down from anybody. He played against Lew Alcindor at the time. He matched up against Wilt Chamberlain. My dad would go head-to-head with those guys.

"He was undersized. He was 6′8″ and played a face-up game. But because he was so physical, often-times he would match up against the toughest player. He would go toe-to-toe with them. I think his style of play reflected Buffalo a lot. He was a hard-working player. Every timeout, he ran off the court. He was the first to the bench.

"He tried to set a good example of hard work and play," his daughter added. "If my dad had a late night the night before with the guys, he was up at 5 a.m. running six miles. He never stopped. He was just a committed athlete. He was also a gentleman. He would sign autographs. He had all the patience in the world with the fans. They were important to him. He never treated people as second-class. He always had time for them."

And that's how I remember him as well. Back at Guilford, there wasn't a bigger man on campus than Bob, yet he was sweet and friendly with everybody.

Bob's career as a player was sadly short. Hip prob-lems forced him to retire at 28, from the Atlanta Hawks. After that he coached the Detroit Pistons for a year and then returned to the Hawks' front office before leaving the game for other work. (If memory

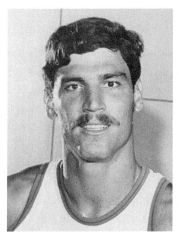

Bob Kauffman

serves, Bob was the GM for Detroit when they hired
Dick Vitale as coach.)

My favorite testimony to Bob's value as a player
was uttered by his coach at Guilford, Jerry Steele.
After Guilford's play-by-play announcer Carl Scheer
told Jerry that Catawba College guard Dwight Du-
rante ("the best 3-point shooter you never saw") appeared that week in a Sports Illustrated piece, Jerry
replied, in his usual slow drawl, "Well, Dwight Du-
rante may have his picture in Sports Illustrated, but
I've got Bob Kauffman's picture in my bedroom."

. . . The best lives have the best consequences. I'd
like one of Bob's to be a celebration of his place as the
Clippers founding all-star — who also happened to
be a four-star dad."[25]

CLARENCE "BIG HOUSE" GAINES

We called him "Big House" Gaines — a leader in sports for the CIAA (Central Intercollegiate Athletic Association Conference) and head basketball coach at Winston-Salem State University. His achievements are notable and worthy of being a legend in sport. "House" as he was called, was a very strong coach and a leader in his conference. His national presence was a miracle for all to see. He was the District 26 NAIA chairman and ruled with a heavy hand.

My favorite "Big House" story involved the game no one was supposed to see. At Guilford, we had number 44, Bob Kauffman, perhaps the best basketball player in the country. He was later drafted number one by the Seattle Supersonics of the NBA.

"Big House" had Earl "The Pearl" Monroe, one of the all-time greats in college basketball. Both were formidable opponents and because of segregation, the two had not met to entertain basketball fans. "Big House" called to invite me to a game no one could see — Kauffman vs. Monroe. Clarence said we could come to Winston-Salem and our teams play each other but no one would be in the gym on his campus. No one could see the game, the parking lot and gym would be empty. No one, he said, absolutely no one. Because of segregation, no one but the two teams would be in the empty gym — absolutely no one!

We agreed to come to Winston-Salem and play before an empty house with absolutely no one but the two teams. I thought it was a great idea and I agreed. When our team arrived at the gym, we saw a strange sight — the lights were on in a crowded parking lot and the gym was packed with a sellout crowd.

Needless to say we knew this was "Big House" Gaines' night — and what a night and what a game! Somewhere I remember Bob Kauffman had scored 55 points and Earl "The Pearl" Monroe scored 54. It was one of the greatest games ever played between two super players — what a treat for all to see. Bob Kaufman, Number 44, was perhaps the best basketball player in the country, as reported by one newspaper. He was later drafted number three by the Seattle

"Big House" Gaines had a strange impact on me for many years, and to tell the truth he still does. We were contemporaries during the days and later became close rivals as athletics directors at rival colleges. I admired "House," as he was called by friends and rivals alike. He was, as they say, "a wheeler and a dealer." "House" showed his ability as a sharp dealer, with which he could easily make a living at Las Vegas behind any gambling table. So it was said when he set Guilford College up. He was always making deals that sounded benign on the surface, but always had a benefit for him personally. Guilford College went from that game to Kansas City, Missouri, to vie for the National Championship.

The story is true and one we could never forget. It was friendly but still is remembered. We are sure the game will never be forgotten by all who saw a truly classic game.

DELORES "DEE" TODD

"Dee Todd didn't plan on being a pioneer. Things just turned out that way."[28] Her professional life has been a series of "firsts." She was the first Assistant Commissioner of the ACC, she was the first African American woman to appear on a Kellogg's Corn Flakes box in 1980, and the first African-American athletics director at A&T University in North Carolina.[27] Not to mention she was the coach for the 1999 U.S. women's track team that went to the world championship. She has been making headlines her whole life in some way, shape or form. Dee Todd has been named Coach of the Year

Delores "Dee" Todd on a box of Kellogg's Corn Flakes[30]

multiple times, including by the ACC in 1997, in Big Ten in 1983, and three times by Georgia State in 1985–87. Todd has been inducted into the CIAA (Central Intercollegiate Athletic Association) Hall of Fame and the Winston-Salem State University Sports Hall of Fame.[27]

Delores "Dee" Todd

"Coaching, however, has been Todd's never-ending passion. Perhaps it's genetic. Her uncle is legendary track coach Dr. Leroy Walker, former chief of the U.S. Olympic Committee [who coached the sprinter Norman Tate, who went on the Goodwill Tour to the Far East with me].

[When asked] Q: What do you admire most about your uncle, Dr. LeRoy Walker? [she said] A: Well, he's seen more and forgotten more than most people know. He has this ability to get up and captivate audiences, and his talks are based on his own experiences. That's a special talent."[28]

A short but humorous story about Dee Todd: I liked to send my sport management majors to "The Atlantic Coast Conference offices" for internships. Dee Todd was an assistant commissioner for the ACC. Her responsibilities included supervising the officiating for baseball as well as planning and directing cross country, indoor/outdoor track and field, and baseball championship events. So if I had a student who was interested in any of those activities, I would ask Dee to consider an internship for them. Her practice was to interview the student in her office and make a decision.

One day one of my students showed up at her door. Before he could walk in she said, "Are you one of Herb Appenzeller's students?" The students replied he was. Dee told him to get out of there and not come back! He had shown up very underdressed for the interview, and she did not like that.

RESOURCES

1. *Pride in the Past*, pp. 93–94.
2. *Pride in the Past*, pp. 114–118.
3. https://www.guilfordquakers.com/history/Profiles/Haskins-_P_E?view=bio
4. http://www.wifmradio.com/OnAir/Gary.aspx
5. https://www.mtairynews.com/archive/15521/view-full_story-16304480-article-pilot_mountain_mayoral_candidate-gary_york
6. https://www.guilford.edu/news/2017/05/remembering-guilford-giant
7. *Pride in the Past*, pp. 96–98.
8. http://www.highpointpanthers.com/news/2009/8/3/MBB_0803090217.aspx
9. http://www.greensborosports.org/guilford-county-sports-hall-fame/jerry-steele
10. https://www.ncshof.org/jerrysteele
11. *Pride in the Past*, pp. 113–114.
12. https://www.guilfordquakers.com/history/Profiles/Harrison?view=bio
13. https://www.guilfordquakers.com/history/Profiles/Kuzma-_D?view=bio
14. NCSHOF May 5, 2017 induction banquet pamphlet, page 68.
15. *Pride in the Past*, pp 88–92.
16. https://www.guilfordquakers.com/history/Profiles/Odom-_D?view=bio

17. http://greensborosports.com/2008/10/29/dave-odom-to
    -work-with-guilford-college-alumni-athletics-as-assistant-to
    -the-president/
18. https://gocuhawks.com/hof.aspx?hof=106&path=&kiosk=
19. https://www.guilfordquakers.com/history/Profiles/Surface-D
    ?view=bio
20. *Pride in the Past*, p. 111.
21. https://www.greensborosports.org/guilford-county-sports-hall
    -fame/tommy-grayson
22. *Greensboro News and Record*, Sunday April 23, 2017.
23. https://winstonsalem.prestosports.com/about/hall_of_fame
    /Hall_of_Fame_Bios/Mary_Garber_Bio?view=bio
24. http://greensborosports.com/2009/01/26/do-the-people
    -remember-these-guys-carr-kauffman-kuzma-free/
25. https://blogs.harvard.edu/doc/2015/07/30/remembering
    -bob-kauffman/
26. https://www.greensboro.com/q-a-with-assistant-acc
    -commissioner-dee-todd/article_e0ad2c25-f37c-5568-b348
    -a41ab08bd1ad.html
27. https://winstonsalem.prestosports.com/about/hall_of_fame
    /Hall_of_Fame_Bios/Delores_-Dee-_Todd_Bio?view=bio
28. https://www.greensboro.com/q-a-with-assistant-acc-
    commissioner-dee-todd/article_e0ad2c25-f37c-5568-b348
    -a41ab08bd1ad.html
29. https://www.nytimes.com/2008/09/23/sports/23garber.html
30. http://yesweekly.com/dee-todd-first-african-american-woman
    -to-appear-on-kelloggs-corn-flakes-box-to-keynote-empowered
    -girls-of-nc-4th-annual-high-tea/

CHAPTER 8

:::::

JACK JENSEN

Jack Jensen was a tremendous coach, teacher, and friend. His many honors and accolades are staggering in the sports realm. Jack played on the 1961 ACC Conference Championship team for Wake Forest under the legendary Horace "Bones" McKinney. He is one of the most decorated coaches in the history of Guilford College athletics, having coached basketball and golf for over 45 years.

After taking over the head coaching position in 1970, Jack led the basketball team to Guilford's first NAIA national championship in 1973. He then went on to coach three more national championship teams in golf. Jack won 386 basketball games in 29 seasons as head coach. He also earned national coach of the year.[1,2]

To relate a personal story about Jensen's character, he was a man of faith and prayer, but one time there was an incident that was very out of character for him. I recall one time passing by the locker room where he was giving a talk to his players after a game. To my surprise and shock, the man who I had never heard use a curse word before was cursing a blue streak. Then, to top it off, he prayed at the end of his talk! The next day, I called him into my

Jack Jensen

office and told him that I heard him cursing the night before and was surprised he had done so. Jack with genuine feeling, stated he did not realize that he was cursing during his talk, and that it would not happen again.

I believed him, and in the years that followed, I never heard him do it again, and his players reported to me that he stopped doing it after that. He was a man who kept his word, who had integrity. For his incredible record, the basketball gym is named for him at Guilford College, with his name written on the hardwood floor.

I wrote the following dedication to Jack Jensen in my book *Ethical Behavior in Sport* after he passed away. It was from the heart, and emphasizes how personally Jack influenced each and every one of our lives at Guilford:

> Every so often, a person comes along who touches the lives of countless numbers of people without fanfare or publicity. This was Jack Jensen, golf and basketball

coach at Guilford College for 45 years, who was a role model for ethical behavior in life as well as in sport. Jack, in a quiet, modest and humble way, exemplified all that is good in sport today.

When a local coach lost her husband to an unexpected heart attack, she took time off to take care of her duties at home. At Jack's recent memorial (having suddenly passed away in May 2010), she told me of the day she returned to school and, opening the door of her classroom, found Jack standing there with a rose in his hand and words of encouragement.

We never knew that the parents of a close friend at Wake Forest University invited Jack to live with them when he coached at the local high school. The husband died and the wife developed a serious illness. She lived a lonely life so Jack traveled 110 miles to bring her roses two or three times a month.

When one of our former basketball players suddenly died of a heart attack, Jack immediately got in his car to be with the grieving family in Atlanta. He stayed for several hours to comfort the family and then left to make the six-hour return trip home. When a former basketball player had his leg amputated after a motorcycle crash, Jack was the first to see him prior to and after surgery, and stayed in close contact in the ensuing years.

Story after story was told during the record crowd memorial service in Alumni Gym [the "Crackerbox" at Guilford College], where his teams played and won exciting and often nail-biting games, and took him to a NAIA National Basketball Championship in 1973, with three members later playing in the NBA.

It was much after that championship I asked Jack to take on an impossible task of reviving a defunct golf program. He was very reluctant but said he would go home and talk to his wife, Marsha. After much consultation Marsha encouraged him. The rest is history: the Golf Association of America installed Jack into its Hall of Fame in January 2008 (one of six Halls of Fame) for a career that included 26 national tournament appearances and four national titles, making him the second coach in NAIA history to win two national championships in two major sports: basketball and golf. After Jack's passing, his grief-stricken golf team lost the Division III National Tournament by one stroke! However, the Guilford College Golf Teams won the league-record 17th Old Dominion Athletic Conference (ODAC) Men's Golf Championship in 2018. What a legend!

All who knew Jack Jensen feel that they are better today because he touched their lives and made a difference. *Ataque in perpetuum, frater, ave atque et vale!* Until eternity, Jack Jensen, hail and farewell, and thanks for a life well-lived![3]

1973 BASKETBALL TEAM: NATIONAL CHAMPS

The rise in women's basketball began in 1956 and is also remarkable and one others continue to find hard to repeat. In 1970–1971 both the men's and women's teams won the ODAC Conference championship. Quite a feat for a school that did not have athletic scholarships until 1962 when Dr. Purdom made his famous run over to save the program. Success breeds success, and all sports began to have winning records at Guilford College after we obtained scholarships.

The 1973 National Championship team had four players that would later go on to the NBA: M. L. Carr, World "B." Free, David Smith and Greg Jackson.

M.L. Carr

M.L. graduated that year with academic honors in history after defeating Maryland-Eastern Shore in the 1973 NAIA title game. He was drafted by both the Kansas City Kings (NBA) and the Kentucky Colonels (ABA).[4]

> He spent his first two professional seasons playing in basketball's minor leagues and Israel before joining the ABA's St. Louis Spirits in 1975. When the ABA folded, he was drafted by the Detroit Pistons and spent three seasons there before signing with the Celtics in 1979. He spent his first two professional seasons playing in basketball's minor leagues and Israel before joining the ABA's St. Louis Spirits in 1975. When the ABA folded, he was drafted by the Detroit Pistons and spent three seasons there before signing with the Celtics in 1979. He led the league in steals and was a Second Team All-NBA Defensive Team selection in 1979. Carr played on the Celtics' 1981 and

M.L. Carr

1984 championship teams and retired in 1985. He spent 21 years with Boston's organization, serving as head coach, executive vice president and director of basketball of operations in his tenure. Also a member of the NAIA Hall of Fame and the Guilford College Athletics Hall of Fame, Carr is president and chief operating officer of The Dream Company, LLC, an insurance marketing company in Huntsville, Ala. He remains an active part of Guilford's community, having served on its Board of Trustees and as tri-chair of the school's successful Our Time in History capital campaign that netted over $56 million.[4]

Lloyd "World" B. Free

During his freshman and sophomore years at Guilford College Lloyd Free received almost every honor you can receive in college basketball. When the Quakers won the NAIA National Basketball Championship in 1973, Free became the only freshman ever to win the coveted Chuck Taylor MVP Award and was named to the Honorable Mention NAIA list for All America honors.

I taught Free and was one of his admirers. I asked Free if he planned to try out for the NAIA World Cup Team. Free, with his wide grin, said, "Coach, what's this trying out? I will make the team without a doubt." Not only did he make the team and played in Cali and Bogota, Colombia, in South America but he was named the Most Valuable Player in the World Cup of Nations Tournament against such opponents as the Soviet Union, Panama, Cuba, Puerto Rico, Colombia and Mexico. Free made the NAIA All America in 1974 and 1975. Free was drafted by the Philadelphia 76ers in the second round of the 1975 NBA draft.

An occurrence was that Free called Coach Jensen to tell him he had an offer from a friend, his agent, who was going to buy him

Lloyd Free

a white 1975 Lincoln Continental. World would pay him back after he signed a professional contract. Jack told him that there was no way he could do that. "People think because you are so good that we are cheating. If you bring back a new Continental they will be convinced of it." World drove an old Plymouth back and was angry for some time. Coach Jensen unselfishly recommended that Free must be receiving "under the table" payments. Nothing was farther from the truth since Guilford had such bad records in athletics. Jack knew how valuable Lloyd was to the Guilford College team but if he were to get injured he might never be drafted, so Free signed a contract bonus that was worth about $250,000.

> Selected by the 76ers in the second round (23rd over-all) of the 1975 NBA Draft, Free poured-in 17,955 points over his illustrious 13-year career, which ranks 49th all-time in NBA history. The prolific scorer from Brooklyn spent four years with the 76ers (1975–78, 1987), while also making stops in San Diego (1978–80), Golden State (1980–82), Cleveland (1983–86)

and Houston (1987). As a member of the 1979–80 San Diego Clippers, Free put together his best season in the NBA. He averaged an astounding 30.2 points over just 68 games, which landed him a spot in the 1980 NBA All-Star Game. He appeared in 886 games over his career, averaging 20.3 points while dishing-out 3.7 assists per contest.

Free was inducted into the New York City Basketball Hall-of-Fame in 1997, joining the likes of former teammate Kareem Abdul-Jabbar, Billy Cunningham, Connie Hawkins, Lenny Wilkens and Nate "Tiny" Archibald.[6]

This final quote sums up Free's amazing contribution and ability to the 1973 team: "As a freshman he led Guilford's basketball team and helped the team win the NAIA National Championship and was named MVP of the NAIA Tournament."[5] His jersey has been retired at Guilford College.

Greg Jackson

Gregory Jackson was reared in Brownsville, NY. As a boy he played basketball at the center when it was the Boys Club. But he was living with family members who were addicted to drugs and was in danger of going that route himself, Representative Edolphus Towns, an old friend, who was then working as a hospital administrator as well as counseling young people in Brownsville, arranged for young Greg to move in with his parents in Chadbourn, N.C., and attend high school there.

After graduating, Jackson went to Guilford College in Greensboro, N.C., where he played with the future N.B.A. stars M. L. Carr and Lloyd B. Free (who later changed his name to World B. Free) on a basketball team that won the 1973 National Association of Intercollegiate Athletics Championship Tournament. Drafted by the Knicks in 1974, he played one season in the NBA. as a guard for the Knicks and the Phoenix Suns. He later played for the Allentown Jets in the Eastern Professional Basketball League.[7]

After pro ball, Greg returned to Brownsville where he became the director of the Brownsville Recreation Center where he grew up to make a difference with the people he loved. Greg later was given the title of the unofficial mayor of Brownsville. Greg passed away in 2012 and the Center was named for him in 2015, the Gregory Jackson Center for Brownsville.[7]

These were the men who helped win the national championship, only 11 years after Dr. Purdom saved the athletic program from extinction! And 11 years after scholarships were given to athletes, Guilford rose to the top to win the national basketball championship! Incredible! That was an unbelievable year and an amazing program to be a part of.

Once again the fact that the Guilford Quakers had four players in the NBA is truly unbelievable: M.L. Carr on the Boston Celtics, Lloyd "World B. Free" on the Philadelphia 76ers, David Smith on the Houston Rockets, and Greg Jackson on the New York Knicks. Quite a feat for a small Quaker college in Greensboro, North Carolina!

This team as a whole has been honored in the Guilford College Sports Hall of Fame.[8]

Golf: Keith King

A native of Virginia, Keith was an All America in basketball and golf at Guilford College. Only ten of Guilford's athletes have earned All America in golf twice, and Keith King is one of them.

At 6' 10", Keith lettered in basketball for two and a half years at Guilford, averaging over 10 points and five rebounds a game. In golf he still holds the school record for the lowest 18 hole game — 66. Under coach Jack Jensen, Keith placed second and helped the golf team attain second in the 1985 NAIA National Tournament. He hit his first score of 66 in 1984, which won the Sam Houston State Invitational in the Bahamas, his one and only collegiate individual title. He also earned District 26 and All Conference honors in 1983 and 1985.[9]

I remember a true account of an event that revealed his character. Keith qualified for an opportunity to earn a position on the pro golf team. Keith hit a tremendous drive to start his way on the par four hole. The crowd shouted about his drive and believed that this super drive ensured a par for birdie. But Keith was so honorable and full of integrity. Even though he was playing for the chance to get on the tour in golf, he came back and said "Oh no, the ball moved before I hit it." No one saw (that hit) but him, but that made him lose his chance to be on the tour that year.

Later on he did get on the tour, due to his good character and golfing ability. In fact, Keith has won many PGA Middle Atlantic tournaments, including the 1990 Tournament of Champions.[9] Today Keith lives in Virginia Beach, Virginia, with his wife and family, and is the head golf professional at the Cavalier Golf and Yacht Club.

SPORTS WRITERS, ANNOUNCERS AND SIDS OF GUILFORD

The SIDs at Guilford (sports information directors) kept the coaches as well as the newspapers and TV stations updated on the statistics, highlights of the games and the athletes at Guilford. Other famous announcers and broadcasters also helped to publicize the athletics at Guilford, which brought familiarity and recognition to the College.[10] Dave Walters is the current SID at

Guilford, one of a line of talented individuals who helped Guilford share the praise its athletes were due.

David Owens

David was a Guilford College public relations director. He also worked for the *Greensboro Daily News*, and was a WWII Army veteran.[10, 11]

Lee Jacobson

Lee Jacobson wrote for the school newspaper while he was a student at Guilford, from 1953 to 1958. He was in charge of public relations for the college, always upholding the cause of the student-athlete.[10]

Woody Durham

Although Woody Durham did not go to Guilford, he followed the Guilford teams as well as other area colleges for WFMY-TV, a local news channel. Woody was their sports broadcaster and also announced Guilford sports on the radio in the 1960s. Woody traveled with the sport teams for the Quakers.

Later he went to his alma mater, University of North Carolina Chapel Hill. Covering Carolina games has been a treat for him over the past 34 years. "Since 1971, Durham has broadcast more than 1,500 UNC football and basketball games and is an authority on all things Carolina blue."[12] He was recently quoted as saying, "I have fun with this job, but it's something I take very seriously. When people listen to our broadcasts, we're sort of the connection between the people of the state with Carolina."[12]

After my book *Pride in the Past* came out in 1987, I saw Woody at a North Carolina Sports Hall of Fame event. He came up to me and said, "Herb, I am not in *Pride in the Past*. Guess you didn't think I deserved mentioning." I was really mortified because of the strong role he played early in Guilford College athletics and I had simply forgotten him. Our travels to games at C.W. Post in

New York were especially memorable. Woody helped with the media paying us more attention. I was determined to make it up to him by not forgetting him and including him in this book.

[*Editor's note*: Unfortunately Woody passed away 3 months after Herb did in 2018, before the publishing of this book.]

A. J. Carr

One of Guilford's more popular SID's and its first student SID, A.J. Carr has made a career as a long-standing sportswriter. A.J. came in 1961 to Guilford "after a successful three-sport athletic career at Wallace-Rose Hill High School where he was an All-State 2-A Tournament basketball player" to become Guilford's sports publicist.[13]

After A.J. graduated, he moved to Raleigh and worked for the Raleigh *News & Observer*. Here is a quote about A.J. that may help one better understand his long career and character:

> Reporters who spend four decades in one department are rare. But while some other reporters moved to editing, to other papers, or to other careers, Carr loved his role and covered some of the monumental events in the history of Triangle [Raleigh area] sports. He wrote about N.C. State's run to the 1974 NCAA basketball title, dozens of ACC Tournaments and Duke's national basketball title in 2001.
>
> He relished writing about lesser-known athletes and would spend as much time crafting a story about a tennis player as a top basketball star.
>
> Carr, quiet and unassuming, has been respected by the people he covered, who appreciated his determination to be fair and devotion to accuracy. He also has a strong history of sports in the market and for

A. J. Carr   A. J. Carr and Herb Appenzeller

years was known for his "Where are they now?" series
that profiled former athletes.[14]

A.J. has been inducted into the North Carolina Sports Hall of
Fame in 2014 and the Guilford College Athletics Hall of Fame.

From his interest in sports coverage at Guilford and writing
for the Raleigh *News and Observer*, A.J. went on to have an illustrious career in sports writing, becoming "one of North Carolina's most accomplished sportswriters."[15] This next quote shows
much about how his personality and character enhanced his career in sports coverage:

> Big-time coaches aren't known for their tact or pa-
> tience. Many distrust reporters, believing they are
> out to get them. It's true reporters get paid to ask the
> hard questions, the ones fans want answered. Carr
> thrived in that environment. He could ask the hard
> questions, but he did it in a way that endeared him
> to players and coaches. He spoke softly, with humil-

ity, and was always polite. His religious faith — he's been an active member of Millbrook Methodist Church for years — is vital to him and influenced his work. Duke coach Mike Krzyzewski said players and coaches sensed Carr's sincerity and commitment and opened up to him. "When you talk about honest, trustworthy and good, A.J.'s picture comes up," Krzyzewski said when Carr retired.

. . . Also when Carr retired, Terry Holland told [the Raleigh *News & Observer*'s] Chip Alexander: "Most of us would settle for the kind of inscription that could easily be his epitaph: 'Here lies the nicest, kindest man you could hope to meet . . . and a darn good sportswriter.'"[15]

One of the best things said about A.J. Carr was this sentence: "He had a gift for writing about athletes as people."[15] That is indeed a gift that not many people have. It is easy to dream about or envision athletes as somehow superhuman people, that they are detached from everyday life and do not go through the same trials and struggles we all face. They however are people just like we are. They do go through some unique struggles as athletes performing in the spotlight, but they still have thoughts, feelings, passions, hopes and dreams like we all do. This was something A.J. Carr had the gift for, the ability to capture an athlete's heart like few can or could.

Ted Malick

Ted was Sport Information Director for Guilford from 1966 to 1970, and later became SID for the Carolina Cougars (a short-lived team from 1971–1974 in Greensboro). Ted passed away early in his career, leaving a life unlived. He was later honored by the NCAA (National Collegiate Athletics Association) for his "outstanding devotion to sports" at the professional and collegiate level.[10]

William Buckley

Bill Buckley "has the distinction of being Sport Information Director at Guilford when Guilford won their first national basketball championship in 1973," the year he graduated.[10] He used brochures, radio broadcasts and sports programs to attract the attention of fans and the public.

Carl Scheer

Carl Scheer's career is connected to legendary player Bob Kauffman, during his beginnings at Guilford College. The work of broadcaster Carl Scheer helped to show others that a small private school in North Carolina could become a national power. He could not have picked a better or more promising player to follow than Bob Kauffman, whose career helped to put Guilford on the map, so to speak. The following excerpt says it best about Carl's career:

> The announcer [for Bob Kauffman] was Carl Scheer, known today as a legendary NBA executive, former GM of the Carolina Cougars, Denver Nuggets, LA Clippers and Charlotte Hornets — and the inventor of the Slam Dunk Contest, among other distinctions. If it weren't for Bob [Kauffman], Carl might still [be in] Greensboro. Suzanne Dietzel in *Greater Charlotte Business* [writes]: "After a respectable run in undergraduate college basketball and baseball, Scheer graduated from Marquette Law School and began a career in a small law firm in Greensboro. After realizing that his desire to litigate cases would likely be un-realized due to the size of the firm, he visited Guilford College and asked to be slated to broadcast basketball and football games — a passion he had indulged in graduate school."
>
> According to Scheer, "Guilford was embarking upon an aggressive, small college basketball cam-

paign, largely driven by star player, Bob Kauffman. I had announced his college career, and once he found himself in demand by two competing leagues, he asked me to represent him for his contract negotiations." Scheer elaborates, "In 1968, agents were unheard of. Knowing I was a lawyer, Bob asked me to represent him . . . .the experience introduced me into the world of sports and business; I was hooked."

Not surprisingly, Carl's work ethic and comfortable personality helped to foster good rapport with team owners, and he was asked to interview for the position of assistant to the commissioner of the NBA . . . . "It was a dream come true. I moved to New York and began my indoctrination into the game. There, my sports career started."[16]

There is a humorous story that relates Carl's broadcasting for the Guilford Quakers. The night Guilford won against Appalachian for the chance to go to the NAIA National Championship in Kansas City, Carl Scheer, caught up in the emotion of the happy fans in the room, accidently misspoke when he said into the radio microphone, "And, Quaker fans, there isn't a dry *tear* in the gym tonight!"[17] (emphasis mine) It took years for him to live that one down.

Johnny Moore

Johnny Moore, was a Student Information Director at Guilford, and interestingly was both an SID and on the track team at the same time. He covered Guilford sports from 1974 to 1977. He "started his sports information career at Guilford, where he handled publicity efforts for the Quakers' eight varsity teams. ... [He later] spent two years as the NAIA District 26 SID office and was the publicity director for the 1974 Poultry Bowl football game and the NAIA National Indoor Track and Field Championships."[18]

From there he went to Duke University where he worked in sports information and marketing until 1990. He has remained connected to Duke through his prior company Moore Productions, Inc. and working for Blue Devils IMG Sports Marketing.[19] He has written two books on Duke basketball.[20] Moore has been inducted into Guilford's Sports Hall of Fame.[18]

Johnny Moore

Wilt Browning

According to his N.C. Sports Hall of Fame bio:

> Wilt Browning of Kernersville was long considered one of the southeast's premier sports writers and columnists. Browning was named the state's Sports Writer of the Year five times (in 1982, 1985, 1988, 1990 and 1993).
>
> A native of South Carolina, Wilt attributes part of his early success to the advice of his first sports editor, Bob Hurt of the *Daily Capital* and *State Journal* in Topeka, Kansas. He was working for the *Journal* part-time while serving in the U.S. Air Force. Hurt told Browning, "When your bosses ask you if you can do something, your answer ought to be 'Yes' because you can do anything that needs to be done in a sports department." He says he has never forgotten the advice.
>
> Browning went on to become the first major league beat writer for the *Atlanta Journal* and covered the Atlanta Braves through the team's first six seasons

in the South (1966–71). He broke the first story in which Hank Aaron said he had his sights set on Babe Ruth's home run record.

Browning later spent five years as the public relations director for the Atlanta Falcons and one year in the same capacity for the Baltimore Colts before moving to Greensboro to become a sports columnist and sports editor for the Greensboro *News & Record*. Throughout his career he also wrote sports for the *Charlotte Observer*, the *Greenville* (S.C.) *News*, and the Asheville *Citizen-Times*.

He retired not long after serving as the sports editor and columnist for the *Citizen-Times*. "My own feelings in retirement now are that I was among the lucky ones who worked through the most wonderful time to be a sports writer, especially in North Carolina. It was a golden era now mostly gone because of changes in newspapering and the manner in which newspapers collect and display sports stories."

Browning considers his days in the newspaper business "the best of times." He is a member of the South Atlantic League Hall of Fame and the author of seven books, many of them about athletes and coaches.

One of his favorite remembrances is Aaron's admission that he had taken exception to what he considered unfavorable remarks by the Braves' radio play-by-play announcer. According to Browning, the famed slugger told him, "If they'll (the Braves' front office) get that guy off my back, I'll go after the home run record." Says Browning of his career: "I don't know that I always succeeded, but I never backed away from any newspaper task." He has been committed to other tasks as well, including serving as president of the N.C. Sports Hall of Fame in 2007 and 2008.[21]

Dennis Haglan

Dennis Haglan began his coaching career at Guilford College after completing his degree at The College of William and Mary. He wanted the Guilford head coaching job when it became available in the early 70s but I felt we needed a clean sweep in football and went outside to bring in Henry Vansant. I told Dennis if Henry left he would be the only candidate considered. That happened and Dennis's selection was greeted with approval by students, faculty, alumni and friends. Dennis was the 19th football coach in 71 years of football. For their outstanding play resulting in 6–3–2, a turnaround record, Dennis earned Carolinas Conference, NAIA District 26, Area VII, and Kodak College Division Coach of the Year! [22]

Dennis Haglan

In addition, Guilford was chosen to play in a post season bowl, the Poultry Bowl in Jamieson Stadium at Grimsley High School in Greensboro. They played another Quaker college, William Penn of Iowa. According to most it was the wettest day in years. Playing a very good football team, the game ended in a 7–7 tie, but was decided by the number of first downs and Guilford was declared the winner. Guilford College football had won its first bowl game in 1931 against Moravian 12–6, while being coached by John Anderson. The 1975 team missed having an undefeated season by four points. "The trip to the Poultry Bowl represented a massive improvement, since they won more games that season than the last eight years of Guilford football combined." [22]

Charlie Forbes

Charlie Forbes was an assistant to Dennis Haglan before he became head coach in 1979. Charlie went on to become the winningest football coach in Guilford history up to that time. He had "7 straight non-losing seasons" from 1979 to 1986.[23] The Quakers had an "inability to score in years past . . ." until Charlie amassed a career record of 57–56–2.[23]

Charlie Forbes came into my office one day at the beginning of the 1984 season, and he closed the door and sat down.

He began with, "You know, Dr. A, I have never told you a story about our chances."

"I know and I appreciate that," I replied, puzzled at his words and where he was going with this lead-in.

"Well, you know our defense is injured, but what you don't know is that our backs have not won a scrimmage against our own team. I don't think we can even beat _____."

I advised him not to mention this concern to anyone. Our first game was against opponent Lenoir-Rhyne. After Guilford won 31 to 15, in a fine display of offense, I met a grinning Forbes at midfield, shook his hand and said, "Charlie, I'm glad you never tell me a story."[23] The season progressed with some wins and losses but a record of 7–3 and Guilford ranked 18th in the final national polls.

When Dr. Rogers came to Guilford as its new president, he decided to take Guilford a step back in athletics: the athletes could not get athletic scholarships, but only need-based grants. We joined the ODAC Conference, which did not allow member institutions to provide athletic scholarships if they were to compete in the conference. I did not wish to go into the ODAC Conference, but the decision was made in spite of my input. Upon much reflection, I decided to retire as athletics director, a position I had held for 31 years. I continued teaching at Guilford until 1993.

Charlie Forbes and Dennis Haglan both operated under the ODAC Conference rules of no scholarships allowed for member schools. Yet without them, somehow, someway, Charlie Forbes achieved the near-impossible: scoring more touchdowns in his coaching seasons than all the years combined and becoming the winningest coach in Guilford's football history.[23]

Mary Broos

The whistle blew. The snap was counted. "Hike!" The football players rushed forward. Down one player went, clutching his knee after the play was over. To everyone's shock, a short, petite, blond woman with a medical bag ran to his side and began asking him what happened and addressing his knee injury. With his tall frame bent over,

Mary Broos

leaning on her shoulder, he limped off the field and to the bench. That short woman — the certified athletic trainer — was Mary Broos.

Al Proctor, often known as the "Father of Sports Medicine" in North Carolina, put forth the practice to have certified athletic trainers on the sidelines to care for injured players in North Carolina. During his time he taught over 5,000 students to become certified athletic trainers. He has been inducted into the North Carolina Sports Hall of Fame for his efforts. Athletic trainers are now an indispensable part of any sport team, and they are trained in the prevention, treatment and management of sports-related injuries. Mary Broos became one of his students. She started earning accolades right from the start of her career. Upon graduation, she was the first woman in the state of North Carolina to become an athletic trainer.

Mary Broos went to work in the Thomasville School System as a teacher and trainer. Later, Al Proctor suggested she go to Guilford College, because he knew Herb Appenzeller, the athletics director there. He knew Guilford would take her when no other schools would because no females were in that business. Al Proctor even called me and asked me if I would consider hiring Mary. I responded that I would, and asked for him to send her down for an interview. Charlie Forbes remembers introducing Mary to me at the North Carolina Coaches Clinic.

Prior to that time, I, unbeknownst to Al Proctor, had requested that the College Administration allow me to find an athletic trainer for the college. According to the school's records, there had not been a certified athletic trainer working at the school in 89 years! With nearly 300 athletes at Guilford College, I knew that they needed someone with professional medical training to watch out for the students. The new school president, William Rogers, agreed and granted permission for the athletic department to search for an athletic trainer in 1980. When Al Proctor called me, it was a godsend.

With Mary Broos' help, the student-athletes were well cared for and looked after. While at Guilford, Mary was given the Athletic Trainer of the Year award in North Carolina. From that honor, the awards came in and she entered Guilford College's Sports Hall of Fame as well as the Guilford County Sports Hall of Fame. In addition, the honors kept coming in from many sources.

Mary later built up a tremendous network in the State of North Carolina and other states. She also was on the national speaking list of athletic trainers to conduct seminars and conferences. Mary became a very active trainer at Guilford College and also gave her services to all who needed help.

Mary has attracted many strong and capable athletic trainers who get advanced degrees. She is a leader of athletic trainers on every level and one of the best most respected athletic trainers anywhere.

In 1984 she also went to the Olympics and represented Guilford College as an Olympic athletic trainer. She truly is a legend in her own special way.[24]

Jerry Hawkins

In addition to hiring Mary Broos, Dr. Jerald Hawkins, an exercise physiologist, joined the Guilford staff as Director of Sport Studies and Coordinator of the Sports Medicine program. Hawkins was a national lecturer and author of many articles on sport medicine, as well as a certified NATA trainer. He and Mary averaged 20 student trainers a year and helped the entire athletic program.

Jerry Hawkins

Jerry has over 35 years of experience in science and physical education. He first obtained a bachelor's degree in health, recreation & physical education from Carson-Newman University in 1967. Jerry then received his Master of Physical Education from The University of Memphis, graduating in 1971. He then received his Doctor of Education from the University of Georgia in 1975. Jerry's average day was 90% teaching and 10% research.

Jerry is the retired Professor Emeritus of Physical Education and Exercise Studies from Lander University. He is the recipient of the 1990 South Carolina Association for Health, Physical Education, Recreation and Dance College/University Physical Educator of the Year Award. He is also the recipient of the 1998 Lander University Distinguished Professor Award, the 1999 South Carolina Governor's Professor of the Year Award as well as the 2005 SCAHPERD Scholar award.

Jerry has over 35 years of experience in science and physical education and is a fellow of the American College of Sports Medicine. Dr. Hawkins serves an expert witness for personal injury cases for individuals. Jerry and I traveled together to speak about injuries and lawsuits in sport management and sport medicine.

One year we went to Lake Placid to speak. The powers that be decided that Jerry and I should not room together and put us each with a couple of their administrators who were terribly loud snorers. When Jerry and I met for breakfast each of us had the same story to tell about not having slept a wink due to the snoring. By the time we finished telling our snorer stories we were laughing hysterically as we did each time we met. Needless to say when Jerry returned for several years he had a room to himself!

When Jerry was awarded the South Carolina's Professor of the Year Award he invited my wife Ann and me to attend. Governor Jim Hodges was in office at the time and the presentation was elaborate. In addition, there were billboards across the state with Jerry's picture. It was quite an honor that we were privileged to attend along with Jerry's wife Sandra and family.

Gayle Currie

Gayle Currie set a standard that any coach would find a challenge to emulate. In 12 years as volleyball coach

Gayle Currie

her cumulative record was 247–161 with Conference Coach of the Year honors three times and District Coach of the Year, once. In tennis her 10-year record is 146–33, with Coach of the Year honors in the Carolinas Conference four times; District Coach of the Year, five times; NAIA National coach of the Year, 1981; and ITCA Coach of the Year in 1984. She has coached six NAIA All-America's in tennis and five NAIA Academic All-America's in volleyball, tennis and basketball.[25]

Gayle coached for 19 years at Guilford and became the athletics director for four years after I retired. She led the 1981 tennis team at Guilford to its first NAIA national championship the first year of its existence, which established Guilford as a powerhouse in tennis. Gayle is the first female recipient of the Guilford College Hall of Fame.

Kerry is the 3rd from the left.

Kerry Kennedy Garris

Kerry Kennedy came to Guilford College as a sports management major and a strong tennis player. I was surprised when she came by my office one day to tell me she was going to transfer to Clemson, where she would receive a tennis scholarship. As a Division I school, she would be the recipient of a full athletic grant. Since we were a Division III non-scholarship program, we could not provide athletic grants.

I remember telling her I understood her dilemma, but I encouraged her to think it over first. However, if she so chose to go, I wished her well at Clemson. Later that day, Kerry returned to tell me she planned to stay at Guilford — what a surprise and good fortune. Little did I know what a gem she was and how happy I would be later over her decision. I had no idea of the honors she would earn over the next four years.

The 1981 Tennis Team

One situation proved Kerry's ability to play under pressure. In our District 26 championship, Kerry injured her ankle and had a difficult time in her tennis match for the championship but won the district championship. Kerry looked forward to the healing process that would take place on her trip to the Nationals. This was the very first year the NAIA National Collegiate tennis tournament came into existence, in 1981, and our team was excited and proud to be allowed to go.

At the Nationals, she won her matches until she reached the final round where she had trouble with her footing. Unable to run, she was prepared to withdraw from the match. The Quakers needed Kerry's win to win the NAIA Championship and it looked bad. Gayle Currie, Guilford's coach, called Kerry aside and told her, "You have the rest of your life to rest up or you can go and play with pain for the national championship. Get out and give it a try — I have faith in you, Kerry."

Playing as hard as she could, Kerry won her match for her first All America and Guilford tennis won the NAIA championship under a miracle-like performance. Kerry earned her first All America and a national championship under the pressure of a painful injury. Because of her performance and courage, she influenced three other women on the team to earn All America honors in such a remarkable way — Shirley Dunn, Sue Ireton, and Leesa Shapiro, with Tammy Strickland earning honorable mention All America.

The 1981 women's tennis team as a whole is in the Guilford College Sports Hall of Fame. Other women on the 1981 team included Lili Carpenter '84 and Stacy Cook '83. Kerry and four other women on that team (Carpenter, Dunn, Ireton, Strickland) were inducted into the Guilford College Athletics Hall of Fame individually.[26]

Kerry Kennedy's honors in tennis while at Guilford College, from the book *Pride in the Past*:

> In 1980, she won All State and All Conference.
> In 1981, she achieved All Conference, All District, and All America.
> In 1982, she achieved All District and All America.
> In 1983, she won All District, NAIA All America (Singles and Doubles), NAIA District and Conference Female Athlete of the Year.

Three All Americas, three years in a row![27]

The Rest of Kerry's Story

Kerry Kennedy married Clark Garris, one of the Garris boys from South Carolina who had two brothers, Steve and Wayne, all of whom played football for Guilford College. Clark, the oldest, was a good linebacker, while Steve was the tough defensive end and cornerback. The three brothers were starters on the football team and helped the Quakers win more games than they lost during their years on the football team.[27]

Kerry has been a flight attendant with American Airlines where she flies regularly to England. A few years ago my wife Ann and I planned a trip to London for a few days. When we sat down in our seats we were told that we would have to change our seat to first class. As we prepared to move we were told that a lady had to use our seats because she became ill. We agreed to stay where we were assigned in second class. However, we kept being served and treated to first class food and drink and were given a bottle of champagne to take to the hotel. As we left the plane, we were told that all this came from Kerry to honor us. What a nice surprise!

A Stellar Performance 31–0: Tarja Koho

Tarja Koho (a native of Finland) was unable to attend the National Tennis Tournament in England because there was no opening. At the last minute, she came to Guilford to compete as a freshman on the Guilford Division III tennis team.

Although she did not play on the famous 1981 tennis team at Guilford, her honors were outstanding. The freshman from Finland played against athletes who were ranked number 1, and she defeated everyone. It did not matter who she played against. In 1982 she won every match she played that year, and went 31–0 to win the championship! She became the first Guilford athlete to become the NAIA national singles champion — an incredible record that has never been beaten since at Guilford![28]

In 1982, she won All Conference, Carolinas Conference Player of the Year, All District, District Player of the Year, NAIA Singles Champion, and NAIA All America (Singles and Doubles).[27] She also was mentioned in *Sports Illustrated* magazine in the "Faces in the Crowd" section for her accomplishments.[29]

She only played with us for one year, sadly. She was very home-sick and so went back to Finland after winning the championship singlehandedly. With her incredible ability in tennis, we believe she had the capacity to go far.

Calvin Hunter

Calvin Hunter has a tremendous record at Guilford College. One of the best quarterbacks in the history of Guilford College, he set 13 records while here. He earned the nickname of "Poise" by his teammates for his incredible poise in the pocket under defensive pressure.[30] Calvin became one of the national offensive leaders in 1990. In 1991 when he led the Quakers to win the ODAC league (Old Dominion Athletic Conference) and was named the league's player of the year, as well as earning Guilford's English Athletic Leadership Award that year. He graduated from Guilford in 1992. Although I had ended my career as athletics director, I still continued to teach for five more years until 1993. Calvin was a student of mine whom I have continued to mentor through the years.

While obtaining a master's in sport management from Georgia Southern and then later a doctorate from the prestigious United States Sports Academy, Hunter coached six years at Guilford, leading them to win the ODAC league in 1994 and again in 1997. In 2017, Calvin Hunter has returned to his alma mater, not as a coach but as an associate professor in Sports Management.[30] A member of Guilford College's Hall of Fame, Hunter still holds three football records out of his original 13 to this day.[31] His experience in teaching at Flagler University and coaching and teaching at Catawba provides a great background in the area of sports management.

Tony Womack

Although Tony played one outstanding season of football with the Quakers, his game was baseball. During his only football season under coach Charlie Forbes, he played with Guilford quarterback Calvin Hunter, and became one of the nation's leading kickoff returners that year. In baseball, his batting average was .337 with 37 stolen bases under coach Robert Fulton. He was awarded with the 1991 Best Undergraduate Male Athlete Award and the 1992 English Athletic Leadership Award from Guilford.

When I was athletics director at Guilford, Tony Womack was a star on our baseball team. He had a habit of pointing to Heaven to honor his late father. Whenever he hit a homer or stole a base, he would point to Heaven.

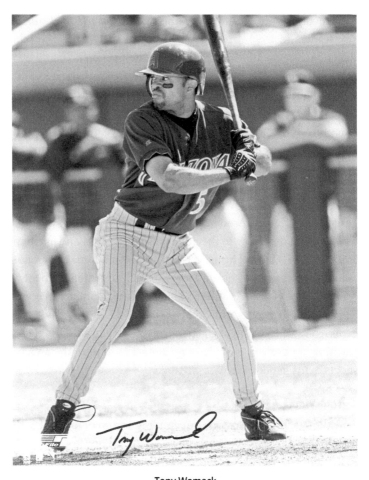

Tony Womack

Tony was drafted by the Pittsburgh Pirates before his senior year at Guilford. I worked with Tony to complete his degree by doing an internship with the Pirates while playing for them in the minor leagues. Later he became a major leaguer in 1993 with the Pirates, becoming their second baseman in 1997.[32]

Tony played for 16 seasons in the major leagues, with some impressive records on his part. He played in the 2001 World Se-

Tony Womack, Herb, and Calvin Hunter, at the Guilford College
Hall of Fame Induction.

ries with the winning Arizona Diamondbacks against the New York Yankees. The Guilford College Athletic Sports Hall of Fame states that "the *Wall Street Journal* noted Womack's game-tying double in the ninth inning of the Series' seventh game against New York as the most significant clutch hit in the Major League's postseason history."[33] He also led the league in stolen bases three times, known as a "three-peat," which included the same year his team won the World Series. He is in the Guilford College Sports Hall of Fame. Today while enjoying his baseball retirement Tony has mentored his own son, Alsander ("Al") Womack, who is an outstanding second baseman entering his third season at Norfolk State in Virginia whom Tony believes will be far better than he.

RESOURCES

1. https://www.ncshof.org/jackjensen
2. http://www.greensborosports.org/guilford-county-sports-hall
   -fame/jack-jensen
3. From the dedication in the book *Ethical Behavior in Sport* by
   Dr. Herb Appenzeller, written in 2011.
4. http://greensborosports.com/2012/01/05/guilfords-m-l-carr-73
   -inducted-into-n-c-sports-hall-of-fame/
5. http://greensborosports.com/2009/01/26/do-the-people
   -remember-these-guys-carr-kauffman-kuzma-free/
6. https://www.nba.com/sixers/community/world_b_free.html
7. https://www.nytimes.com/2012/05/03/nyregion/greg-jackson
   -brooklyn-youth-mentor-dies-at-60.html
8. https://www.guilfordquakers.com/General_Releases/2013
   -14/13Hall
9. https://www.guilfordquakers.com/history/Profiles/King-K?
   view=bio
10. *Pride in the Past*, pp. 215–223.
11. https://www.greensboro.com/out-of-county-obituaries/article
    _e4bc1dc6-752e-51ae-8b6f-b8e5282b1127.html
12. https://www.ncshof.org/woodydurham
13. https://www.guilfordquakers.com/history/Profiles/Carr-
    _A.J.?view=bio
14. https://www.wralsportsfan.com/college_basketball/story
    /4831095/
15. https://www.ncshof.org/ajcarr
16. https://blogs.harvard.edu/doc/2015/07/30/remembering-bob
    -kauffman/
17. *Pride in the Past*, pp. 124.
18. https://www.guilfordquakers.com/history/Profiles/Moore-J?
    view=bio
19. http://www.goduke.com/ViewArticle.dbml?ATCLID=211515979
20. http://www.durhamsportsclub.com/2017/04/4517/
21. https://www.ncshof.org/wiltbrowning
22. *Pride in the Past*, pp. 155–156, 158.

23. *Pride in the Past*, p. 204.
24. *Pride in the Past*, p. 170–172.
25. *Pride in the Past*, p.179–180.
26. https://www.guilfordquakers.com/history/Profiles/Tennis_Team_-80--81?view=bio
27. *Pride in the Past*, p. 263.
28. https://www.guilfordquakers.com/history/champion
29. https://www.si.com/vault/1982/05/24/627999/faces-in-the-crowd
30. https://www.guilfordian.com/sports/2018/02/09/calvin-hunter-joins-the-colleges-faculty/
31. https://www.guilfordquakers.com/history/Profiles/Hunter-C?view=bio
32. https://www.greensboro.com/pretty-in-pinstripes-former-guilford-college-star-tony-womack-has/article_53af3529-9cff-58f6-a519-99a6ea0f59a2.html
33. https://www.guilfordquakers.com/history/Profiles/Womack-T?view=bio

CHAPTER 9

THERE IS LIFE AFTER GUILFORD!

After I retired as athletics director in 1987, I taught Sport Law
and Risk Management for four more years. I gave my second
commencement address in 1992, my other being my first year
at Guilford College so that Mr. Brown and Mr. English could
"show off their Latin major athletics director." In 1993 I retired
from Guilford as the Jefferson-Pilot Professor of Sport Studies
Emeritus. Along the way I had gotten to know Dr. Frederick
Mueller, who was a professor and former Department Chair of
Exercise Science at the University of North Carolina. His work
as the Director of the National Center for Catastrophic Sports
Injury Research resulted in a book: *Football Fatalities and Catastrophic Injuries, 1931–2008.* With my field of sport law and risk
management it was a natural to have a chapter in that book and
I recently completed a chapter for Mueller's second edition entitled "Risk Management Strategies for Football." As a result of our
relationship, Fred asked me to teach a sport law class in the Sport
Exercise graduate program at Chapel Hill and I did so for four
wonderful years. I had taught graduate courses for the University of North Carolina at Greensboro also for a number of years,

Conducting a risk review on proper use of a football helmet.

mostly in the summer, but this was a unique opportunity for me to teach in my field in graduate school.

While at Guilford College I developed a sport law newsletter named "Sports and the Courts" along with an attorney from Winston-Salem, Tom Ross. After a successful few years I was attending a conference in Florida when an energetic young man came up to me and said he knew all about me and he would like to conduct risk reviews of college and university sports programs as to the safety of their programs, thinking that, as a lawyer, he could help keep the programs out of court. I did not know him at all but he convinced me to try after he set up risk reviews for the University of Miami and the University of Oklahoma and we would do a 70–30% split with regard to payment. After we started out so well, I said 50–50% and we have worked together for the past 32 years! Ron Baron is his name and we have had many ventures and adventures since we met. His mother once told me I was the only person Ron stuck with in his life!

In 1989 we started a new newsletter "From the Gym to the Jury," named after my first book which was a result of my doctoral dissertation at Duke University. The prestigious Michie Company in Charlottesville, Virginia was my first publisher. They published all the law books at that time used by attorneys around the world. My book was certainly different but they continued to publish my next six books until they were bought out by LexisNexis

Some of my books!

in 1989. The Michie Company suggested I talk with Keith Sipe at Carolina Academic Press in Durham, North Carolina. They have produced the rest of my books including this one and we have become lifelong friends with Keith and his wonderful wife, Linda Lacy.

Todd Seidler

After I retired, I retired (or so I thought and always said I would do). Todd Seidler was hired to become the coordinator of the undergraduate Sport Management major at Guilford College after I retired. Joyce Clark, director of intramurals and a physical education professor, called me repeatedly to come meet Todd and I was not interested. Then one day she called to say they were at The Village Tavern restaurant and had a place for me at lunch. What a mistake I had made and what a mistake it would have been as Todd and I have been the closest of friends and professional colleagues since that day. The only problem was that Todd only stayed at Guilford two years! He had told the search committee that he would only leave if a position opened at the

University of New Mexico and it did! Todd assumed the role of department chair of the graduate program in Sport Administration at the University of New Mexico.

Todd Seidler

Todd has been very active in an organization called Sport and Recreation Law Association, serving as the executive director of SRLA for many years and also president. It just so happened that I had been at the inception of that organization some 30 years ago. It has become my most helpful professional organization as well as where my best professional friends congregate. I was very fortunate to have SRLA establish an award named the Herb Appenzeller Honor Award for outstanding service to SRLA in 2014.

Three of my favorites among others have received the award: John Grady, Associate Professor, Department of Sport and Entertainment Management, College of Hospitality, Retail and Sport Management, University of South Carolina; Annie Clement, retired as a member of the graduate faculty at the University of New Mexico; and Anita Moorman, professor, Health

Anita Moorman

and Sport Science at the University of Louisville. I was so honored to receive three presidential awards from these SRLA presidents: Todd Seidler, University of New Mexico; Rebecca Mowrey, Professor of Wellness and Sports Sciences, Graduate Program Coordinator at Millersville University; and Anita Moorman, Professor, College of Education and Human Development, University of Louisville.

Annie Clement

Annie Clement, PhD, JD, has been a lifelong friend since the early days of SRLA. She is a true friend and a very sharing professional colleague. She retired from the graduate faculty at the University of New Mexico. We met her when she was the Dean of the Florida State sport management program. We had the opportunity to have lunch with her students, some of whom we have helped get positions in the field of sport management, like John Grady at the University of South Carolina, or offered advice in publishing a book, as with Kadence Otto at Western Carolina University.

Annie has taught at The Ohio State University, Bowling Green State University and Cleveland State University. She also held appointments at the University of Iowa and Florida State University. Her bachelor's degree is from the University of Minnesota, Duluth. She also has a master's degree from the University of Minnesota, Minneapolis, a doctorate from the University of Iowa, and a law degree from Cleveland State University. Dr. Clement is the author of three books, twenty-two book chapters, and over fifty articles and one hundred presentations. Her areas of research are intellectual property, gender equity, aquatics and risk management.

Annie Clement

Dr. Clement, a Fellow of the American Bar Association (ABA), is also a past president of the National Association for Sport and Physical Education (NASPE). Among her national awards are an Honor Award from the American Alliance for Health, Physical Education, Recreation, and Dance (AAHPERD); an Aquatic Council Merit Award; a Joy of Effort award from the NASPE; an ABA Section of Business Nonprofit Lawyers Award; and a Distinguished Scholar award from the Safety and Risk Management Council.

All the while I continued to do risk reviews with Ron Baron and Todd Seidler and a former Guilford student of mine, David Harlow. They encouraged me to continue in the area of expert witnessing, which I did for the remainder of my life, as well as write 29 books and continue publication of "From the Gym to the Jury," the online newsletter, five times a year.

Vaughn Christian

One morning I got a call from Dr. Vaughn Christian, chair of the Health, Leisure and Exercise Science department at Appalachian State University in Boone, North Carolina. Dr. Christian was wondering if I knew anybody who would like to teach sport management and sport law in the graduate program at Appalachian State. After I suggested some possibilities, Vaughn told me he wanted me to take the position!

My wife, Ann, was taking care of our seventh grandson that morning. I called her and said, "Now don't say no!" She asked a few questions and said we could consider it. So after an interview we moved to Blowing Rock, North Carolina, for half a week for the next three years, driving from Greensboro to Boone and back each week! Our neighbors had been renting a condo there and we split the week with them that year and rented it ourselves the next two years. Ann's biggest worry was the possibility of bad weather because it did snow there quite often. Fortunately, we only had one class day where they told us to come home. The graduate students at Appalachian State and UNC-Chapel Hill were outstanding and many have excellent careers today. I continue to hear from them with news about jobs, weddings and babies! It is very gratifying to continue to hear from them.

I had one other interesting teaching experience one summer. I was asked to teach a sport law and risk management course online for California at Pennsylvania University in California, Pennsylvania. One of my former students from UNC Greensboro, Roy Yarbrough, ended up at California at Pennsylvania after leaving Liberty University in Lynchburg, Virginia. Ann agreed to do the online part of the course and we ended up with 40 students. I assigned a risk review of a facility or program of their choice as a final exam. That was a learning experience, to grade 40 papers that had a minimum of 40 pages! We would have taught again online except the pay was the same after the first year of preparation and 40 students were too many!

John Horshok

I met John Horshok because we went to the same barbershop. I had just gotten my hair cut and walked out as John was walking in.

John asked the barber, "Who was that man?" She said it was Herb Appenzeller. John said, "I have been trying to find that man for several years!"

He had heard of me for a long time but did not know how to locate me, and here he found me in person, living in the same town. After reaching out to me, we became professional contacts and good friends. John has been very successful in business ventures and in sports as a manager, which he loves. He also loves to write, having been a sportswriter for many years.

With over 35 years of experience in sport marketing, John has represented numerous and significant business entities in the categories of sports entertainment, businesses and nonprofits. When Coca-Cola—the biggest supporter of the International Special Olympics—asked me to be the National Project Manager, John was the first guy to help develop the Special Olympics with corporate money.

John has won many awards, including being named past recipient of the Joseph P. Kennedy National Sportswriter of the Year award, the U.S. State Department's "Understanding Through Sport Award" and many (awards) specific to newspaper and magazine writing, following his career beginnings as the President of the Michigan Collegiate Press and his first assignment at the Ann Arbor (Michigan) News. John shared the Phoenix Award with Kenny Rogers, Muhammad Ali and Frank Gifford for their Coca-Cola sponsored national award winning spot for the Special Olympics. Joe Theismann and John shared the Majestic/Insight Magazine National Humanitarian Award for work in support of the 1983 International Special Olympic Games. John is a member of the Washington, D.C. Sports Hall of Fame and Fairfax Softball Hall of Fame. While living in Summerfield, North Carolina, he coached numerous youth teams in softball including coaching his daughter, Maggie.[1]

Marty Sheets

A wonderful experience that John and I shared was getting to know Special Olympian Marty Sheets. John's involvement with Special Olympics began when Eunice Kennedy Shriver founded the Special Olympics in 1968. John was on the board and as Marty lived in Greensboro, he had contact with Marty and his father and mother, Dave and Iris Sheets.

Martin "Marty" Sheets, who became a face of the Special Olympics, has won more than 250 medals while competing for more than 40 years in its events. Marty, born with Down's syndrome, competed in golf, swimming, Alpine skiing, tennis and powerlifting at the Special Olympics. He was involved in the first international Special Olympic summer games, at Chicago's Soldier Field in 1968.[2]

Marty Sheets

Marty became ill after arriving there and was unable to compete, but at a banquet concluding the event, Eunice Kennedy Shriver, the founder of the Special Olympics, having learned of his disappointment, walked over to his table.

"I understand you trained to come to the games but you got sick," she said. "Well, Marty, for your guts and your effort, I want you to have a gold medal, too. Here you go. Marty Sheets, the winner of the special gold medal for bravery."

She draped it around his neck.

In the years to come, there were medals aplenty for Marty as an all-around athlete in events ranging from international to local competitions. Seven of his medals came in the Special Olympics World Games. Among his achievements, he captured two medals in skiing at the first Special Olympics winter games, in 1977 at Steamboat Springs, Colorado, and two more at the summer games in Minneapolis in 1991, lifting 225 pounds, slightly more than twice his size.

Marty was named the PGA Tour's 2006 national volunteer of the year for his longtime work helping spectators keep track of players' scores at the Wyndham Championship in Greensboro, North Carolina. In 2013, he became the first Special Olympian inducted into the North Carolina Sports Hall of Fame in Raleigh.[2]

Mrs. Shriver chose Marty as one of five Special Olympians portrayed with her in an oil painting by David Lenz. It was unveiled at the Smithsonian's National Portrait Gallery in Washington in May of 2009, three months before her death.

Marty's father, David, said in a 2015 telephone interview with the *New York Times*, "Through the years, we've had so many people with children or other family members with special needs say how much it's meant to see Marty and know of his accomplishments. He's been an inspiration to them."[2] Marty passed away in 2015 at the age of 62.

Johnny and Jane Roscoe

I have known the Roscoes since they were seniors at Guilford College. After the publishing of my first book I went on many speaking trips. Jane was the sitter for my children and became very close to the family with Johnny accompanying her. Johnny and I also go way back, he as a football player at Guilford College and me his athletics director.

I remember first seeing the football recruit from South Carolina in 1966. With his bright red sweat pants and white shoes, Johnny was the only recruit dressed that way and he stole the show. Four years later he had a serious knee injury. I was surprised to see him limping onto the Lenoir-Rhyne game field. It was his final game in his senior year as a tough but small defensive back. Johnny insisted on finishing his senior year on the field and his courage showed that night when he played under difficult conditions. Johnny helped the Guilford team win in a super game.

One woman I know used to tell everyone who said anything about how wonderful Coach Roscoe was that Herb Appenzeller taught him everything he knows! I appreciated the compliment but felt I had to correct it, as it was simply not true — Coach Roscoe had learned from me but had gone on and become great all by himself with his wife, Jane.

His mantra was "Always be prepared for any change you may have to make on the field in the game." He could adjust quickly because he was prepared. This was his mantra and no one expected less from the diminutive defensive back. Johnny Roscoe coached as he played — tough, dedicated to his players, and winning the right way with no shortcuts.

What is fascinating about Johnny is that he did something that I believe very few people have ever done — he incorporated the strategies of the Confederate generals of the American Civil War into his coaching football. That was one of the things that made him great. He was tough, but he was good. He used the strategies he had read and studied to help him win games. He had an incredible ability to realize what he had to do to come back from behind, and he did it time and time again and won. He is known for his preparation. Prepared he was, actually scripting his games for each player's position.

One of the things that made Johnny successful as a coach for his many teams was his wife, Jane. She became an integral part of his coaching strategy and philosophy. She would spend time with the players at practice to teach them about good manners, virtues and honesty — life lessons. She helped her players and players from

Coach Johnny Roscoe and his mentor, Herb Appenzeller

other schools in their preparation for the S.A.T. The players love her and respect her. She is "Mrs. Coach" to countless athletes. They listened, and it showed. Honestly, her contribution to her husband's teams was just as essential and foundational to the teams winning ball games as was his dynamic coaching and ability to come from behind.

After graduating from Guilford College, Jane and Johnny both became high school teachers in South Carolina. Johnny coached football as well as taught history — and as no surprise, he loved teaching and researching about the Civil War. Jane Roscoe could teach the outstanding students as well as the high risk students with success. Both Jane and Johnny were great influencers on their high school students who appreciated their efforts on their behalf. The two have made contributions in both academics and athletics wherever they have taught or coached.

In 2007, Johnny and Jane asked to come see us. We were surprised when Johnny told us the "dynamic duo" was ready to leave retirement for the position of the first football coach at the newly built Northern Guilford High School in Greensboro, North Carolina. The Appenzeller "Bed and Breakfast" was the scene of much planning, reminiscing and fellowship between a coach and his mentor. We continued to house the Roscoes from day one until today as they moved back and forth to South Carolina.

The story of Jane and Johnny Roscoe at Northern High was one that broke all records. They won the 3-AA State High School Championship in football three years in a row. Many of his players went to college due to Johnny's excellent recommendations, and got placed into great schools. Some of his former players such as Keenan Allen and T.J. Logan went on to the pros. The seasons the Roscoes coached are in the class of Ripley's Believe It or Not or Hollywood At Its Best. It should be reported in its full glory but a lesser account will do. Incidentally, the Roscoes won a Southern Conference championship at Hartsville High School in the state of South Carolina in 2007. It is clear that the duo have set records that may never be broken in high school athletics.

Johnny is a member of five Halls of Fame, in both North Carolina and South Carolina. Jane and Johnny both are in the Guilford College Hall of Fame, as I nominated them as a couple. Johnny was a founder of the South Carolina Football Coaches Association even though he ended his coaching career in North Carolina.

Johnny Roscoe's coaching record consists of the following: from a 4–5–1 record at Forbush High School to a 62–2 at Hartsville High to a 135–106 at Lancaster High School. Then he capped his career at Northern Guilford High School with a 102–12 record and four state championships. Johnny began coaching at Northern in 2007 and left victoriously in 2012. He returned to Northern in 2014 to win his 4th state championship. In 2015 Northern lost in the semi-finals and Johnny retired after that game. The stadium at Northern High is named the Johnny Roscoe Stadium.

The Roscoes achieved the impossible dream while at Northern Guilford when they won their first state championship in North Carolina. Northern Guilford was playing for the third state championship against Charlotte Catholic on the Wake Forest BB&T

Jane and Johnny Roscoe

Field. Charlotte boasted a great fullback named Elijah Hood who was predicted to score many points. On the other hand, Northern had T.J. Logan, a speedy halfback. Both teams predicted they would win. In that game, T.J. scored eight touchdowns and gained 500 yards. Hood ran for less than 100 yards. T.J. broke the State of North Carolina's total offensive record. The Arizona Cardinals publicized that "there is speed and there is T.J. Logan speed" when he was drafted number five for them.[4]

The Roscoes have four Northern men they coached that are in the NFL. Keenan Allen is starring today with the Los Angeles Chargers, as is Maurice Harris. T.J. Logan is with the Arizona Cardinals and Chris McCain is with the Indianapolis Colts, although he did not finish at Northern.

Sports Management at Northern High School

One teaching opportunity arose out of my new friendship with John Horshok. I got the cherished opportunity to teach at

Northern High School. Johnny Roscoe wanted me to teach a sport law course for the Northern students. John and I collaborated to teach along with Reine Thomas, the classroom teacher. We had the opportunity to bring many sport figures to class as well as teach about sport law and risk management. At that point in life I was using a walker and found the students to be so thoughtful and careful with me. Matt Page, particularly, walked me to the car every day and stayed with me until Ann picked me up.

On several occasions, I had the opportunity to speak at Northern High to a group of teenagers multiple nights before their football games. That gave me great pleasure to give them a rousing speech or story to inspire them and give them the impetus to win their game.

One night when they were leaving for a state championship game, which of course they won, I went over to see them off on the bus before we went to the game later. One of my favorite student players spotted me sitting to the side. He rushed over and hugged me, and then the entire team came over and hugged me! I could have played in that game with that motivation!

Ann and I had always thought we could not teach the young people today with the different challenges they face. However I was so impressed with the Northern students and their ability to show affection and tell me that they loved me — I had a wonderful time.

At one such speaking event, I told the team a story I had heard for many years, one of a Marine hero. I had always heard it was a true story, but never knew the man's name. When I was to speak to the team at Northern High, I decided to use that story again...

Sgt. Richard Weaver

For years Paul Harvey, a great storyteller on radio, used to end his broadcasts with: "and now the rest of the story." Jeri Rowe, a columnist for the Greensboro *News and Record*, wrote about a Korean War hero, Richard "Dick" Weaver, on August 2, 2013. I

Sgt. Richard Weaver receiving the Silver Star

want to tell the rest of the story of United States Staff Sergeant Dick Weaver.

Dick Weaver, the son of a pitcher on the Brooklyn Dodgers baseball team, had major league ambitions. All of this changed in a rice patty in Korea on March 28, 1953.

Eighty U.S. Marines had taken a hill and the next morning 800 Chinese soldiers with tremendous fire power came to regain the hill. The 80 outmanned Marines were ordered to leave through the rice patties for safety. As they were leaving, the Marines heard the plea for help from a gravely wounded Marine from Cicero, Illinois. He was crying out in pain for someone to help him to safety. His lieutenant ordered his men to continue their escape because, as he instructed his group, "anyone who goes out to attempt a rescue will sadly be killed immediately."

Platoon leader Dick Weaver recognized the voice of Chuck, his Marine buddy. Knowing the potential of sudden and sure death Weaver handed his rifle to his lieutenant and said "I'm gone." Under heavy fire from mortar shells and machine guns he reached his fellow Marine who cried out — "I knew you would come, I knew you would come." As Weaver was carrying Chuck to safety, he was hit by machine gun fire that almost took his arm off. He placed the wounded Marine on the ground and dragged him 60 yards to a ditch. A helicopter, under heavy fire, rescued the two wounded Marines. Chuck did not make it and Dick spent the next 11 months undergoing a series of operations on his damaged arm.

While coaching at Chowan University I had heard the story of the two Marines. I told my football team the story of an American hero who defied all odds to save a member of his platoon. The story illustrated the virtue of being a member of a team and was well-received by the Chowan squad.

Sixty years later, I told the story to the Northern Guilford football team, coached by my former Guilford athlete Johnny Roscoe. Johnny and his wife Jane always worked together to motivate and inspire their young football players in South Carolina and at Northern Guilford. At the beginning of the 2012 season, going for their third consecutive North Carolina state high school football championship, Jane asked me to once again tell the Marines story.

During the 2012–13 season Ann and I met a neighbor of the Roscoes at the first game, and developed a friendship where we sat with each other as we attended home and away games moving toward the championship.

Dick Weaver was his name. He was the son of a Brooklyn Dodgers pitcher, and was also a great pitcher. The story goes that the Dodgers were returning from spring training and stopped to play a seven-inning exhibition game against a local team on which Dick Weaver pitched. The story is that Dick struck out 18 batters and got three hits himself while at bat — two doubles and a homerun. The future looked great for a baseball career. All of that changed after he went to war.

At the final home practice at Northern High School before the State 3AA Championship at BB&T field at Wake Forest University, I asked Dick to accompany me while I met with the Northern team. I had read materials about this friend who received the Silver Star and Purple Heart after saving a fellow Marine. As we drove to practice, I said to my friend, "You know Dick, your story sounds a lot like the story I am telling the players." Dick Weaver said, "That was me!"

We met with the players, and I gave my motivational talk. At the end of it, I turned to Weaver, pointed at him and said to the players and coaches, "Here is the man I told you about." The players went wild. One of the players was heard to say "There is no way we are *not* going to win this game." The following evening we saw the Northern Guilford Nighthawks win their third State 3AA Championship and complete the first undefeated season for Coach Roscoe.

On the Monday after Memorial Day, I was asked to speak to the Northern Guilford 2013–14 football team along with other area teams at a workshop sponsored by the NFL and the National Guard. A longtime friend of both mine and Dick Weaver, the late North Carolina Representative Howard Coble surprised Weaver with a framed certificate which he introduced into the Congressional Record about Weaver's heroic and inspirational act of courage. A resident of Summerfield, North Carolina, for 33 years, Weaver has finally received the recognition due to his heroic actions in the Korean War.

Health Concerns

I have had diabetes for many years, ever since the team doctor at Guilford discovered it. Having done fairly well with it for many years, including exercising and following my doctor's diet, I started having problems. I remember once being recognized at an event, and my blood sugar dropped so low that I could not accept the award. It was the Order of the Longleaf Pine, the most prestigious award given by the then Governor of the State of North Carolina.

Then in June of 2015, my wife, Ann and I suddenly discovered I had gangrene of the left leg, and I had to make a decision to amputate or not.

My doctor came into my hospital room and said to me, "You have four hours to live. If we do not cut your leg off, you will die in four hours."

I said to him, "Doc, what's there to decide? Cut my leg off!"

To me the decision was simple: I wanted to live, so the leg had to go. The doctor took it off. Unfortunately, that would not be the only time in my life I would have to make that decision.

In January of 2016, I found myself being faced with this decision again. We decided once again to have it done. Both of my legs were now amputated below the knee, and I was given prosthetics for both legs. I slowly learned to walk again, with the help of some wonderful therapists and the aid of a walker. I did go back to games and I still enjoyed them, although the trips were more difficult.

It was at this discouraging time I received so many cards, letters and phone calls of encouragement and support from many friends and family. Having been a member of New Garden Friends Meeting since Ann and I married, we have been "Held in the Light" by Friends and other friends.

Lou Brock

There is one letter I received during that difficult time that stands out to me. It is from a man I never met before in my life, but had heard of for years. His name was Lou Brock, the professional baseball player.

One of baseball's star players was Lou Brock of the St. Louis Cardinals. He made the All-Star team and he became one of the best players in baseball history. Lou Brock had outstanding years with the St. Louis Cardinals.

I recently received a picture of the St. Louis Cardinals' player Lou Brock. The picture was of a smiling baseball player who had earned fame and fortune. Brock sent a 5"x7" photo of himself in his Cardinals uniform. On it he wrote, "Herb, we have something in common! Regards, Lou Brock."

On the back it said, "11-15-2015. P.S. I heard you had a hard time like I did — I was going to sue my doctor but my lawyer said I didn't have a leg to stand on — Best, Lou".

He had a leg amputated, just like I did. He was writing to me in a note to tell me not to worry and to encourage me, with some humor. It was well received and I enjoyed it immensely. I will always appreciate his note and his encouragement.

Lou Brock was one of the finest baseball players to ever play the game. We watched him on television go to the mound at one of the games to throw out the first pitch to start a game — one leg and all. Brock showed the courage he had to never give up, to set an example for people who have suffered amputation(s).

I appreciate his sense of humor, his dedication to baseball and humanity. In this book, we have examples of girls and boys, women and men who have refused to let a disability get them down. We have examples of men and women who suffered amputation who refuse to let a handicap take away their desire to play — whatever their disability. If our readers get little else from this book, the author hopes it will inspire our readers to continue to continue — no matter their condition.

I later found out that John Horshok knew Lou Brock, and had asked him to send a note to encourage me. John is very altruistic. He loves to help others and has a big heart. With people who have done great deeds that are unknown to others, John likes to recognize them publicly for what they have done. He has that kind of heart. Although I met him relatively late in my life, John introduced me to so many people, and tried to show he cared for me by recognizing me in any way he could.

After Teaching

Around 2009 I taught my final class at Northern, ending my many years of teaching. I had taught for 16 years at four institutions after finishing teaching at Guilford in 1993. All together I had been a teacher and professor for 60 years ever since 1949 at Rolesville High.

When I was athletics director at Guilford for all those years, I could rarely go to a Wake game. Now I was free to go and did go to many Wake Forest football games. We enjoyed every minute of our Wake Forest experience.

However, the highlight of my Wake Forest involvement was getting a call from Dr. Ed Wilson, then Provost of Wake Forest University, telling me I was going to be inducted into the Wake Forest Sports Hall of Fame. That was a very emotional call for me as I never expected to be inducted. The ceremony was in January of 2008, the same year I was inducted into the Guilford County Sports Hall of Fame. Ed Wilson's call produced a very emotional response from me, because I never thought it would happen.

Ann and I were truly speechless and became even more so because that same day my neighbor stopped by to tell me that

Project Smile had paid the remainder of his daughter's surgeries for a cleft palate. I had helped my neighbor Mackey Chandler get in touch with them because he had paid out of his pocket for years for his daughter's surgeries. Neither he nor I could talk that day for emotion but I was equally happy about the Wake Forest induction as I was about him being reimbursed for his daughter's medical expenses. I had a younger brother named Bobby who was born with a double cleft palate and endured many surgeries successfully but painfully. He was six years younger than me and died after surgery for his appendix when he was given too much anesthesia. That affected me greatly and I always had a place in my heart for people with a cleft palate. What an emotional yet wonderful day!

Billy Ray Barnes

Of all the people on my list of legends, Billy Barnes is at the top of my legends and I consider him the best one.

Billy, who grew up in Landis, North Carolina, was the best running back at Wake Forest University and I remember going to Charlotte to the Wake Forest–South Carolina game in the final game of the year to see him compete. Billy had a bad shoulder separation and was not expected to play because of the painful injury. The problem was that he only needed several yards to become the first player in the ACC to rush for over 1000 yards. Everyone was saying he would not play, but I knew he would play because I knew what a competitor Billy was.

When the game started Billy Barnes lined up on offense, as no one expected. They just did not know him and his toughness, but they soon learned who he was. The sold-out crowd cheered when he caught the first kick-off. He gained enough ground to beat the ACC record to pieces! That with a bad shoulder! He was tough, boy he was tough. But he is a very likable guy as well.

He won many honors at Wake Forest, including All Conference and All America. He was good at football and baseball also.

He was part of the 1955 baseball team at Wake Forest that won the National Championship — the only team in Wake Forest's history to do so. He was a third baseman, one of their stars who led them to victory.

Billy later was drafted by the Philadelphia Eagles. A Pro Bowler, he later led the Eagles to win the National Championship in 1960 as a great running back.[3] The National Championship was the greatest game to win before the Super Bowl was developed.

He also became part of the Wake Forest Sports Hall of Fame. He got in the Hall of Fame as soon as he was eligible in 1975, which was quick! As an alumnus, Billy Barnes donated money to fund a room in his name at Wake Forest University. He certainly had the money, and he was loyal to Wake Forest, so that is why he donated so much. He never forgot where he came from.

By the time Billy and I became friends, we never played on the same team, I was using a walker. Billy Ray liked it so much I gave him the information so that he could get one for his mother. We really bonded over that and at every home game and Hall of Fame Billy Ray and Ed Bradley, Jr., made sure they spent time with me more because I had been a teammate of Ed's father, Ed Bradley, Sr., who also played in the pros for the Chicago Bears.

It's not easy to pick who is the best, and I am sure that others would pick somebody else. Billy Ray Barnes is my selection, out of all the legends I have listed in my book.

RESOURCES

1. Marketing material (for the new ballpark to be developed in Loudoun County, Virginia), written by John Horshok.
2. https://www.nytimes.com/2015/05/25/sports/martin-sheets-a-decorated-special-olympian-dies-at-62.html
3. http://thesportsdaily.com/2011/03/26/qwhen-the-money-was-relativeq-billy-ray-barnes-and-the-nfl-champ-eagles-of-1960/

4. https://www.azcentral.com/story/sports/2017/05/07/rookie
   -rb-t-j-logan-could-home-run-threat-arizona-cardinals
   /311741001/

5. http://npg.si.edu/blog/eunice-kennedy-shriver-1921–2009

EPILOGUE

:::::

By Wilt Browning

THE LEGENDARY HERB APPENZELLER

I have been tempted more than a few times to write a book about Dr. Herb Appenzeller. Each time the thought seems the most daunting of my writing career and each time that thought has popped up in my mind I have finally pushed it back for one simple reason:

I know Herb Appenzeller too well.

Now, I understand that one could take that as other than complimentary, as though I knew something about the man that would make the oaks on the picturesque campus of Guilford College shake to their roots. Or something salacious enough as to leave the Quakers quaking. The truth is the exact opposite. I know how complex the man is, yet how kind, how accessible and how brave which makes writing on the subject very difficult: where does one begin?

One could begin on the day the president of the school hired Herb away from Chowan College to be the Quakers' football coach. His hiring came with an ultimatum, as does that of most college coaches. But Herb's may be only one of its kind in all of college athletics. Herb had stood to leave the office of the president and reached to shake hands with his ultimate boss.

"Mister Appenzeller, one thing more," the soft-speaking president said. "When your team is on the field, I hope your players will show gentlemanly manners to the other team, and keep those boys in mind, too."

Guilford's new football coach was astonished. "Do you mean, sir, that if we can beat the daylights out of a team, don't do it?"

"Why, yes, my good man. That's exactly what I mean." Herb's first team at Guilford beat the daylights out of no one, winning but a single game, perhaps making his boss very pleased.

To this day, no coach in any sport at Guilford College has ever been fired for losing athletic contests. That tidbit of the Appenzeller legend could make a wonderful first chapter. But so many other parts of his life could stand that test as well.

For example, there was an early season practice session that would portend something other than a losing season. Coach Appenzeller had put his team through the paces early, and yielded the field to the Green Bay Packers who were scheduled to play a pre-season game within the week at Winston Salem. Herb, still in his football practice pants of the time, hurried back to the field to watch Vince Lombardi pace back and forth as Bart Starr, the great quarterback, put a team loaded with future NFL Hall of Famers, through their paces.

Standing at a distance on the sidelines, Herb was transfixed by the football talent on the football practice field at Guilford College. He hadn't noticed the school president approaching until his boss put a hand on Herb's shoulder and also stood silently watching the team on the field.

As usual, the Packers wore their world-famous helmets with the "G" for Green Bay on each side, one of the early great logos of football.

Seeing the "G", the Guilford College president stood there for a time. As he departed he congratulated Herb on the talent he had put on the field that day.

"Well, my good man, it looks as though we're going to have a pretty good team this year." Herb was left momentarily speechless. Yet in the years yet to come, Herb would become the person to whom team coaches at Guilford would come for consolation or advice when things weren't going well. If necessary, he would remind each one that no coach at Guilford College had ever been fired for losing. It would not start with Herb, then the school's athletics director.

One could make that the opening chapter of a book.

Old Wake Forest graduates who matriculated at the Baptist college before its move to Winston-Salem would get into such a book quickly if there were stories of D.C. "Peahead" Walker, himself a legend of some consideration.

Some of those stories, one in particular, include Herb. Walker won more football games at Wake Forest than any coach until Jim Grobe came along and tied his record of 71 victories. One of those victories for Walker came against South Carolina in 1946 in the first Gator Bowl football game.

During civic club speeches, Herb has occasionally pointed out that he set a Gator Bowl record in that first game that stood for more than half a century and which many considered close to unbreakable.

Herb had not been a starter for the Deacons that day, but stayed reasonably close to Walker as the coaching legend growled and fussed his way to a 26–14 victory over the Gamecocks. Herb didn't exactly shadow Walker, but he stayed close enough to be sent into the game at the sweep of the old coach's hand.

On his first play, Herb took a pitch on a pass play, paused for a moment, set his feet and threw the football in the direction of a receiver he thought was open.

He wasn't. But South Carolina's Dutch Brembs was there picking off Herb's pass at the Gamecock ten-yard-line and returning the interception 90 yards for a touchdown. Herb and Brembs thus were locked in a shared Gator Bowl record that stood for decades. He can handle that sort of thing and other slings and arrows of life. Such as the night of his induction into the North Carolina Sports Hall of Fame, a flower girl obviously not fully versed on state sports, called to "Doctor Appenzooler" to come have his lapel flower pinned to his suit coat.

That story perhaps could get us into this man of great faith, a gentle spirit, and a generous personality. But so many other memories would work as well.

Courage could be spelled Appenzeller. It wasn't aching, gimpy knees from his own career as a football player that would have laid low a lesser man. He has for years now been the victim of Type 1 diabetes.

In his late 80s, the sinister blood disease ate away at the man, taking toes first, then a foot, later a leg to above the knee and finally the other leg in the same fashion. As he had as a player and a coach, Herb still fought with bravery and at an age when learning something new is difficult, he spent time learning how to make prosthetic legs work reasonably well. There was never a give-up spirit in the man.

Even his honeymoon was no simple matter. When Herb married Ann, the two decided to make a trip to Appenzell, Switzerland, the ancestral home of the Appenzellers. The trip was memorable for more than one reason. The train to Appenzell had begun slowly to move as the Appenzellers hurried to hop aboard. Herb pushed Ann safely aboard along with their luggage. But he didn't make it, falling near the wheels of the rolling train on the rough scrabble supporting the track. He suffered many injuries.

But during a long hospital stay to recuperate in Appenzell, many natives of Appenzell visited his bedside, including even Croatian soldiers recuperating from the war. He returned home battered but forever thankful for the hospitality of the people of Appenzell.

Actually, not many people perhaps know how Doctor came to be affixed to the front of his name. Maybe the book could begin there.

Herb is a proud man. Proud of his service to his college as both football coach and athletics director. Proud that *Pride in the Past* has long been the Bible of the financially limited athletics at Guilford. Proud that he spent much of his life in academia.

It was in the academia portion of his life that his pride began to become an issue for himself. Again and again, Herb over the years represented the athletic department at faculty meetings. It was a room headed, of course, by the college president and attended by dozens of men and women, all of whom were doctors of something, and one non-doctor Herb. He came to feel that he was at a disadvantage when it came to his "uneducated" role as a mere coach and administrator. One way or the other, Herb decided he would change that perception.

He enrolled in a doctoral program at Duke University, an impressive outpost of academics as prestigious in that regard as Guilford College. Doctorates in Sports Administration were not available in those days, but Herb would have chosen something somewhat suited to the intellect of a football coach. Herb made his choice of courses.

Latin!

Herb could have found a way to study folks such as John Heismann or Pop Warner or the Four Horsemen of Notre Dame. Nope. He took the road less traveled, studying all the classics and an ancient language which would have been reasonably foreign to all the doctors sitting around the room at faculty meetings.

May we introduce Doctor Herbert Appenzeller? He had succeeded in a way that became more important in his sports career at Guilford than merely as a way to thumb his own nose to the stogy professors. To this day, it is common for Herb to offer sought-out wisdom in Latin, English translation to follow. And any athletic team ever called together in pre-game rituals to listen to the inspiration of this legend of a man always were offered phrases in Latin that applied to trying hard to win.

And in all the years that were to follow, Herb became a national authority for athletic entities across the nation in risk loss assessments and investigations. He has authored more books, mostly on risk management and law as it applies to sports, perhaps than all the professors then serving at Guilford, and still was writing this one beyond the age of 90. Many coaches and athletic administrators turn to an Appenzeller volume when confronted with questions of the causes and consequences of injuries to both athletes and fans. Many of the most noted athletic stadia and arenas in the nation have sought an assessment by Herb in an effort to spare the expense of litigation.

Those of us who know him well just call him Doctor A. A legend needs nothing more.

— Wilt Browning

Steve McCollum of Guilford's publications and sports information office wrote the following, which honored Herb after he retired in 1987 as athletics director from Guilford: "How do you pay tribute to someone who defies all limitations? Herb Appenzeller is a man who cannot be contained in such a small space as this."

INDEX